THE
PRACTICAL
GUIDE
FOR
NEW LAWYERS
WINNING STRATEGIES FOR CHANGING TIMES

Steven E. M. Hartz

ISBN: 1-4392-4025-6
ISBN-13: 9781439240250
Library of Congress Control Number: 2009904454

CONTENTS

FOREWORD

The idea for this book began to take shape a few years ago. As I looked at my own career and the careers of other lawyers I knew, I began to see how valuable it would have been in the early years to have had a greater, and earlier, insight into the essential techniques that lead to success in the legal profession. As times have changed, I think the urgency of this book is greater than ever. The legal market is difficult to navigate today. New lawyers need every competitive advantage they can find to succeed. At a moment when they feel most challenged, or even helpless, they need to be empowered to develop and enjoy their careers.

I need to thank many people for their support over the years. My mentor at the University of Chicago Law School and longtime friend, Thomas Stillman, first taught me the practical skills of good lawyering as he supervised my work at the Mandel Legal Aid Clinic. His own dedication to the cause of justice and legal excellence has always inspired my career. He was kind enough to review a draft of this book and to make many valuable suggestions.

Former colleagues at Cleary Gottlieb Steen & Hamilton deserve my eternal thanks. As a newly minted associate, it was a pleasure and an invaluable learning experience to watch them practice law. More recently, Lee Buchheit of that firm has been kind enough to share his ideas on legal writing with me.

James Honkisz, former in-house counsel at Coca Cola, kindly read a draft and offered some insightful suggestions.

My cousin Joseph Feinberg, a talented graduate assistant at the University of Chicago, offered me some important ideas on writing skills.

To my many former colleagues in the U.S. Attorney's Office in Miami and at MFY Legal Services in New York City, I owe the greatest respect and thanks. Working tirelessly, under staggering caseloads, they have fought for a better society. Their many skills and achievements have always been both inspirational and instructional.

All of my colleagues at Akerman Senterfitt have taught me, through their own successes, more than I can possibly acknowledge. I debated many of the ideas on law firm economics extensively with my partners Stephen Roddenberry and Jonathan Awner. Nina Whiston, Thomas Ross, Gregory Presnell, Thomas Cardwell, Charles Schuette, Andrew Smulian, Robert Zinn, James Miller, Michael Fertig, James Bramnick, and many others worked with me on various management issues with patience, good humor, and wisdom. Additionally, numerous associates have been good enough to share their lives and experiences with me.

I benefitted greatly from the insights and encouragement of my cousin Jessica Simonoff, who kindly reviewed a draft of the book and has offered many useful suggestions. As a new lawyer, she has offered a fine example of success and real enjoyment of the profession. Her own career—past, present, and future—has inspired much of this book.

Finally, most of all, my wife, Dr. Janice Lindsay-Hartz, offered me great support, as she cheerfully and critically reviewed the book. A distinguished clinical psychologist and pioneer in the theory of emotions, Jan has consistently provided me with enormous insight into the individual dynamics of successful lawyers and the group dynamics of successful law firms.

The responsibility for the content of this book, however, is mine and mine alone. The opinions expressed in the book do not represent the views of my firm or of any of the fine people mentioned above.

January 2010

PREFACE

L et me welcome you to the legal profession. You are about to embark on a career that can give you tremendous personal rewards and enable you to serve others in a meaningful way.

Lawyers have often been the butt of negative jokes and cynical derision. But the truth is that in the world at large and America in particular, lawyers are leaders of society. Cicero, Abraham Lincoln, Franklin D. Roosevelt, Mahatma Gandhi, Nelson Mandela, and countless other great leaders were lawyers whose contributions profoundly influenced the course of history. Over the centuries, millions of other lawyers, whose names will never be remembered, have toiled to create great societies and institutions. You have chosen a truly great career.

Because you have picked up this book, I know that you are the type of person who really wants to get the most out of your career as a lawyer. I promise you that this short book contains proven techniques that you can put to work right away to ensure your peak performance in any legal organization, particularly in the difficult economic times we all face today. At the same time, the book provides enough background information about the legal industry to enable you to make good strategic decisions in your career.

For over thirty years, I have been privileged to work in law firms of different sizes in both the public and private sectors. I worked for several years as an associate in a Wall Street firm. I did a stint in a legal aid office, worked as a federal prosecutor, and then opened my own business as a sole practitioner, ultimately ending up as a senior partner and top business producer in a large law firm. Through trial and many errors, I have come to learn ways in which all lawyers, and particularly new lawyers, can maximize their effectiveness. By studying the most successful lawyers, I have learned the techniques that really give lawyers the winning edge. Whatever your future may hold in this fast-paced, ever-changing profession, the techniques I discuss here will enhance your success and enjoyment of the profession.

Today we face unprecedented economic challenges. These challenges impact new lawyers at a point in their careers when they are least equipped to handle them. Much of this book is devoted to economic issues facing new lawyers and the legal organizations in which they work. Armed with the information in this book, you will be far better attuned to what is going on in your organization and in the legal profession in general. Remember, improvements in your skill and productivity will be critical to your competitive success. At the very least, I promise that you will learn a lot from my mistakes.

In early 2009, many of the most prestigious firms in the country were laying off lawyers and support staff. In most instances, these layoffs were tied to the downturn in financial work. Litigation and other areas of law will, in due course, increase. Thus the *net* change in demand for new lawyers may ultimately be somewhat less than some fear. Also, it is not clear that the entire burden of reduced demand has fallen on new lawyers. Older, less productive lawyers have been equally significant targets for layoffs. For the new lawyer, the challenge is how to stay nimble in the market. The strategies I discuss will help you do that.

More experienced lawyers can also benefit from the techniques and strategies covered in this book. Much of what is good for the new lawyer is good for the rest of us as well. If nothing else, experienced lawyers can always become better mentors if they look at the world through the eyes of their less experienced colleagues.

Apart from fear of the current economic situation, the most common complaints I hear from new lawyers are that they are dumped on, overworked, underpaid, forced to do menial work, and underappreciated. They also suffer from enormous anxiety about their ability to perform their work, office politics, and uncertainty about their future. Many of these concerns, of course, also afflict more experienced lawyers. This has led to high turnover and dropout rates in the profession, among many other problems.

One of the most famous psychologists of our time, Professor Martin Seligman, has studied and analyzed the unhappiness of lawyers.[1] He has found that the root causes of this unhappiness are that (a) law schools have selected us for our ability to find problems, (b) we often develop a feeling of helplessness in the face of professional events over which we think we have no control, and (c) much of our work involves

---

1. Martin E.P. Seligman, et al., *Why Lawyers Are Unhappy*, 23 CARDOZO L. REV. 33 (2001).

"zero-sum" adversarial games in which one side wins at the expense of the other.

You cannot change how you were selected to be a lawyer. But, as Professor Seligman has found, you *can* learn to overcome the pessimism that is prevalent in the profession. I can attest to the fact that from the outset of your career, you will accomplish more if you focus on solutions as well as problems and look at a glass half empty as a glass half full. You can readily gain skills that will always empower you, even when things go wrong. And I am confident that you will find, as I did over time, that the best aspects of the profession of law are collaborative rather than adversarial.

The skills and information set out in this book will reduce the amount of time you spend on the job by improving your efficiency, raise your salary by improving your contribution to your organization, and give you an edge in getting to work on the best projects. I am also confident that following the steps outlined in this book will reduce any anxiety you may feel and strengthen your self-esteem.

Contrary to popular belief, it is not necessary to work an absurd number of hours to be a successful lawyer. It requires a significant amount of time, to be sure. But initiative, motivation, efficiency, teamwork, and economic savvy are far more likely to achieve results. Lawyers who do nothing but bill hours have no time to think strategically or to improve their skills. They wind up maxed out and burnt out. It is not a good place to be.

Also, contrary to popular belief, it is not necessary to have been a super scholar to be a good lawyer. In fact, there is little empirical proof that high law school grades are correlated with success in legal organizations. The evidence is that success in all organizations is generally highly correlated with initiative, interpersonal skills, and personal organization. None of these is especially stressed or measured in law school.

If you got through law school, you are capable of doing great things in the law. Great lawyering is learned behavior. With diligence and instruction, you can do most anything in the law with tremendous success. So if you were just an average student, you can still be a legal superstar. But you can only achieve this goal if you don't give up on yourself. When you walk into court for the first time, nobody will care one iota about your grade in Contracts. The chances are great that they will not even know where you went to law school. And if you have prepared properly, it will make no difference.

I also hope that this book will be of some help to people who have to cope with lawyers. I have tried to present the unvarnished truth about the stresses the profession places on new lawyers. I offer ideas for balancing the stresses, improving productivity, and getting more enjoyment from the profession. I sincerely hope that in the process, families who must cope with lawyers will understand them better and enjoy them more.

Lastly, I want to point out that while this book stresses many aspects of private law firm life, I also comment on other avenues of law practice. My stress on firms is by no means accidental. Well over 50 percent of graduates initially go to work for private firms. Nevertheless, most of the techniques I discuss are readily applicable to any legal organization. While we, as lawyers, tend to calibrate the differences in our jobs with detailed precision, the differences between being a successful lawyer in government, nonprofit organizations, for-profit corporations, and private law firms are not all that great. The qualities of good lawyering are far more universal than we tend to believe.

FINDING A JOB

Let's begin with a few tips on landing your first job.[2] For those of you who already have found a job, I hope that these observations will stand you in good stead as well. You never know when you may want to find a new job, whether by choice or by necessity.

Positive motivation, strategic planning, persistence, and flexibility are required to get a job in any market. Although I am going to speak about these elements individually, they are inextricably and dynamically linked. Without positive motivation,

---

2. A great deal of information about legal placement is available from your law school, as well as from the NALP, the Association for Legal Career Professionals ("NALP"), and Vault publications. My observations are meant to supplement, but not supplant, research you can undertake using information from these sources. Additionally, you should leaf through a copy of GUERILLA TACTICS FOR GETTING THE LEGAL JOB OF YOUR DREAMS by Kimm Alayne Walton (Harcourt Brace, 1999). It has many interesting practical tips on the mechanics of creating resumes and the skills of interviewing. Don't, however, be fooled by the title. As a first-year lawyer, you will not become the senior partner of a large firm by using "guerilla tactics."

you cannot think clearly about approaching the task of analyzing the market for your particular skill set. If you are enthusiastically targeting a market that has no use for your services, you are wasting your time. If you are not persistent in the face of the certainty of many rejections, you will lose your positive motivation. And if you are utterly inflexible in your job requirements, you will reduce the possibility of success enormously.

POSITIVE MOTIVATION

To get a job you have to be positively motivated. If you are not positively motivated, you will not make the investment of time and energy that is required. Prospective employers will pick up on your lack of motivation, and you will lose to any competition you face.

I know that law school has stressed the importance of looking at every troubling aspect of a situation. And I am not blind to the currently dismal state of the market as I write. But, please, even if you are normally a cynical skeptic, now is the time to give it a break. In fact, by reading this book, you are already on the right track.

For most of us, finding positive motivation in the job search has been easy: we needed to pay off student loans! But beyond that, you can find motivation by stepping back and looking at the bigger picture. You chose to get a law degree for some reason. Go back to that initial reason and think about the effort you made and the goal for which you strived. Take a look at the possibilities that the law can offer in your career. Talk to lawyers who enjoy their practice. Read the rest of this book to see how your career can unfold in a positive way. And take some time to enjoy the fact that you are about to leave the boredom of your third year of law school in the past and to get a paycheck for doing something interesting and helpful to others. This moment is the best time of your life.

Ignore the doomsday forecasts about the end of the world and the collapse of the legal market. Given their track record to date, you can be sure that when the pundits predict that we are on the verge of disaster, we are about to enter a period of sustained growth and prosperity. It may take a little longer for some of you to get a job today, but I assure you that you will get a job.

STRATEGIC PLANNING: MARKET ANALYSIS

Whatever you hear about the legal market's problems today—and they are many—the range of opportunities open to new lawyers is almost limitless. You can work in thousands of agencies in the public sector, taking advantage of the many opportunities for important responsibility and personal satisfaction that public service can bring. You may be able to clerk for a judge. You can—and an ever-larger percentage of lawyers do—work in a law firm. You can work in a large firm or a small firm. You can work in a myriad of different specialties. You can teach law. You can work in business as a lawyer or a non-lawyer. So when you are starting out, know that you are sitting at a feast of opportunity, even if jobs are harder to come by and some may be foreclosed by events over which you have no control.

In 2008, within nine months of graduation, approximately 89.9 percent of new graduates had landed a job in the legal profession.[3] It is true that the economic downturn will affect

---

3.   NALP, *Market for Class of 2008 Law Graduates Shrinks,* available at http://www.nalp.org., last visited January 12, 2010. NALP's statistics were based on 43,587 graduates from 198 ABA-accredited law schools. This was down from 91.9 percent in a comparable study of the class of 2007.

this statistic in 2009 and 2010 by lengthening the duration of time needed to acquire a job, but I do not think that the demand for new lawyers will be suppressed for long. Indeed, the promise of more regulation of the financial industry could lead to even more demand for lawyers to craft the regulations, to administer them, and to advise clients about complying with them. From the beginning of the nation, lawyers have been a foundation of our society. The temporary disruption of the economic cycle notwithstanding, a society of laws needs as many lawyers as possible.

If you doubt what I am saying, just consider the price of attorneys in this country. Personal injury attorneys charge as much as 45 percent of the ultimate recovery for contingency fees. Law firms routinely charge $300–$1,000 per hour for lawyers. Even solo practitioners charge $250 to $500 per hour. These high fees are evidence of a *scarcity* of lawyers, not of some vast oversupply.

Many of the recent layoffs of lawyers have been due to an over-allocation of lawyers to finance and real estate due to bubbles in those particular areas of business. The market will reallocate these lawyers to other areas in due course. This reallocation will not occur without some trauma. You can expect that some firms will fail. But the market *will* produce a solution within a reasonable period of time.

The current salary structure of the market for new lawyers is significant. The profession has developed a strange salary distribution in which 42 percent of graduates are starting at under $65,000 per year and 23 percent are starting at $160,000 or more per year.[4] The distribution is largely

---

4. *See generally,* William D. Henderson, *The End of an Era: The Bi-Modal Distribution for the Class of 2008,* elsblog.org, last visited August 15, 2009.

"bi-modal" with clusters at both ends. Additionally, more and more lawyers are working in large firms, and those at the top of the salary scale are almost always working in firms of one hundred or more lawyers.

The bi-modal distribution results from the fact that the top two hundred corporate law firms ranked by size recruit very heavily—almost exclusively—from the top twenty law schools in the country. For these firms, the hiring equation is predominantly as follows:

Perceived labor need + Law school reputation + Applicant grades + Interview = Offer

Under this formula, if you are at the top of your class at one of the top twenty law schools in the United States, you will find work without too much difficulty because there is a large demand for top credentials in the large corporate law firms. If you are not in this group—and that is most of you—don't despair! You are qualified, and you *will* find a job, provided you are positively motivated, flexible, and disciplined.

Remember that regardless of their ability to get your first job more quickly, grades and law school rankings are crude, unreliable predictors of future success. Grades measure your ability to give quick, superficial answers under great time pressure. If grades meant that much in the practice of law, law professors would be the greatest practitioners and would be making millions of dollars exploiting their unrivaled skills. Instead, they lecture year after year for a salary that is less than most of their peers make in private practice. I have supervised lawyers from all the major law schools and lawyers who never went to a great school or attained high academic honors. I have not found a clear correlation between grades and success as a lawyer. Good grades are helpful, but they count for much less in a world where initiative, interpersonal skill, self-organization, and communication ability are critical.[5]

In strategically analyzing the market, I suggest that you search for and target the market to which your services are most valuable. There are opportunities for everyone. If you were at the top of your class at Yale, getting a job is relatively easy. If not, don't get discouraged. Many good law firms do not need graduates from famous law schools. For example, they may do insurance defense work, where the prime qualification is that you have the capacity to become a good trial lawyer. This legal specialty requires hard work, public speaking ability, and interpersonal skill far more than exam-taking or even writing skills. Other law firms may want graduates of prestigious law schools, but do not have the profile to acquire them. Further, alumni of law schools that are not well known may have founded success-

---

5.   I do not, of course, entirely discount the value of grades. They are often "door openers" to highly successful legal jobs. But neither my own experience with lawyers from different backgrounds nor the limited empirical data that exist support the conclusion that grades are critical factors in organizational success. *Compare,* Elizabeth Goldberg, *Is This Any Way to Recruit Associates?,* AM. LAW., August 2007 (describing the findings of a study by a Missouri law firm that examined the relationship between associate grades, law school rank, and school rank to the actual performance in the firm and found that they did *not* predict "who would become a standout lawyer"), and William D. Henderson, *Are We Selling Results or Resumes?: The Underexplored Linkage Between Human Resource Strategies and Firm-Specific Capital,* INDIANA UNIVERSITY SCHOOL OF LAW, RESEARCH PAPER NUMBER 105, April 2008 (describing a two-year study by Bell Labs showing that organizational success was not correlated with cognitive ability), *with* Richard H. Sander, *The Racial Paradox of the Corporate Law Firm,* 84 N.C. LAW REV. 1755, 1794–5 (2006) (describing a University of Michigan study showing that grades were predictive of long-term *financial* success of University of Michigan Law School alumni).

ful firms. In that case, they may know your school intimately and immediately see your potential.

Outside of the law firm arena, you will also find many opportunities that are not grade dependent. For example, at http://www.goarmy.com, you will find that the military is hiring attorneys. Military law is an independent body of law that is highly sophisticated. Lawyers hold officer rank. They are valued in the military for a vast variety of skills. They prosecute, defend, and judge crimes. They prepare and negotiate contracts. They draft wills. I have worked with many former military lawyers. I have yet to find one who was not competent and dedicated. The training they received was excellent, and I never even considered asking what their law school grades were.

Yet if you look at the requirements of the military, they do not stress high grades. The military is looking for dedicated patriots with good physical conditioning and a willingness to embrace military life. They don't expect to fill their ranks with members of the *Harvard Law Review*.

Look at your current skill set and past successes. Identify the areas of your strengths and focus on career opportunities where those strengths will be most valuable. For example, if you are fluent in Spanish, you may want to think about firms that have a strong Latin American practice. Think about trying to get a job with the Immigration and Naturalization Service, an agency that does a lot of its business in Spanish. If you have worked with law enforcement, think about joining the FBI or state law enforcement. Everyone has some strength; play to yours.

It is also worth spending some time analyzing the geographical market on which you are focusing your search. Often the graduates of your law school have such a great desire to remain in the area of the school from which they graduated that they are a glut on the local market. As a result, the local law firms can take their pick of the litter. In other communities, your law school may stand out, and the pool of potential applicants from that school may be much reduced.

Please bear in mind that law firms generally like to recruit from multiple law schools. They will usually have alumni of a variety of schools who want to push for the recruitment of graduates from their schools. Additionally, different schools have different strengths and characteristics. A firm may have had especially good results from lawyers picked from one school or another. There may be political reasons for picking graduates of different schools or a desire to expand the firm's potential referral network. You can try to exploit this need for diversity.

If you have a question about the types of opportunities in the marketplace, check with your career placement office. Call alumni. Talk to professors. People with more experience can help you spot the target market for your situation. You are certainly not prohibited from applying to other markets. But naturally you will want to focus the bulk of your effort on the areas in which you have the best opportunity of success.

PERSISTENCE

It is vital to be persistent. You have to circulate your resume in your target market. Networking is essential. Follow up with phone calls and seek interviews. Be sure to make extensive use of your school's career services department, your teachers, the alumni of your school, and the friends of your family. Let everyone know that you are looking for a job. As often as you have the opportunity, mention your search to practicing lawyers. Believe it or not, most lawyers want to help people get their first job. I can assure you that there is nothing more rewarding for a lawyer than to help new lawyers join the profession. So please don't be shy about asking for help. We are all shy to some degree, but a good lawyer has to get over it. You cannot represent a client well if you cannot represent yourself well.

Without even knowing you personally, I will venture to make a prediction: In the course of your job search, you will be rejected—perhaps more than once. It's a virtual certainty. What is important to realize is that there is nothing personal in it. A job search is, in part, a numbers game. Just keep going. Like baseball, even the best players succeed in hitting only a third of the time.

FLEXIBILITY

I cannot stress strongly enough that to increase your probability of success, it helps to be flexible in the type of work you will do and where you will do it. I have often heard from students that they don't ever want to do personal injury work or some other specialty about which they generally know very little. I also often hear that a lawyer is looking only in a particular city. There is such a thing as being too targeted in your search.

In this market—or any market for that matter—you have to be flexible and strategic. It is most helpful to target a viable potential market for your services, even if it is not your first choice of work, and even if it is not in a city in which you had planned on living. Law is an amazing profession. The great thing about it is that after you have gotten a few years of training on your resume, you can reinvent yourself. Plenty of lawyers have started out in Montana and ended up on Wall Street.

ENTRY POINTS

Let's take a brief look at some of the traditional entry points for the profession. These are not the exclusive entry points by any means, but they are worth examining at the outset because a large percentage of new lawyers start their careers through these gateways.

Judicial Clerkships

Judicial clerkships are a great entry point into the legal profession. They give you a unique opportunity to understand the process of the courts and to hone your research and writing skills. They are opportunities to learn through observation about litigation skills and about different lawyers and firms in the community. They are also a way to develop a relationship with a judge, who ideally can be a mentor during and after the clerkship. However, the downside to clerkships is that firms are reticent about giving full "credit" in salary and seniority for time spent in clerkships, recognizing that many practical skills for working in a law office are not taught in a clerkship. Clerkships of longer than two years can be particularly problematic unless one year has been spent with a particularly prestigious court or judge.

While clerkships in the federal court generally require extremely high grades, many other types of clerkships and internships are somewhat less demanding. Likewise, local judges may want to support local law schools, where they often teach part time. Check with your career services department to find out about opportunities for clerkships.

When picking a clerkship, you should try to find out what role you will be playing. Will the judge take the time to teach you, or will you find yourself relegated to picking up the judge's dry cleaning? Is your judge a respected intellect, or is he or she a political hack? Is the judge cool under pressure, or will you be running around like a maniac trying to fulfill impossible tasks? Can the clerkship lead to a more prestigious clerkship or other employment opportunities?

Your law school should be in a position to help you answer some of these questions. Former graduates are often a good source of information, but you can do some investigation on your own by seeking out former clerks and reading the opinions of the judges. It is amazing how much you can tell about the character of a judge by a close reading of his or her opinions.

Firms

Not everyone wants to be a clerk to a judge. Some cannot afford it. Some simply do not find litigation appealing. In any event, there are not enough clerkships for everyone. A majority of new graduates enter the profession through employment at firms. This is an especially good way to start out in the profession, because it offers some training and money to pay off those onerous student loans. There is also a relatively well-developed process for applying to firms. There are on-campus interviews. You submit a resume. You may get a call-back interview, etc. Hopefully, the process—perhaps combined with networking— will get you some offers. If not, please read on. I will offer some additional suggestions in a moment.

How do you choose a firm? This is perhaps the most important decision you will initially have to make and one of the most difficult.

Most people think they are choosing a firm for the long run. However, this notion is a myth. Most lawyers work at a firm for a few years and then leave. So the first thing to consider is whether working at the firm you select will lead to better jobs in the future. You should try to land a job with the firm with the highest reputation and quality that will hire you. As I said earlier, I believe that you should not initially place geographic or lifestyle considerations ahead of the quality of the firm. You can always move to paradise after you have been trained at a first-rate institution situated in what you consider to be a second-rate location.

Specialists may find perfect training in boutiques. However, unless you are one of the rare lawyers who really wants to specialize from the outset and knows what specialty you want, you are probably better off trying to begin your career by working for a firm with a diversified practice. You will generally create more options by working in a firm that is either large already or seeking to be large.

Of course, all things being equal, it is always wise to consider the financial health of the firm. You may choose to stay at a firm for a long period of time, and its financial health is obviously a prerequisite to yours. Moreover, financially successful firms often get better cases and may offer a more valuable experience than financially unsuccessful firms. In any event, wealthy firms usually, but not always, offer better amenities and a better working environment.

How do you find out about the financial health of a law firm? As I will explain later, all law firms tend to be financially fragile. However, some are clearly better off than others. Finding out about the financial health of a firm is very difficult, if not impossible. However, for what it is worth, here are a few indicators to be viewed skeptically.

First, you can look up the finances of the largest two hundred law firms in *The American Lawyer*. The magazine annually surveys financial statistics of the largest firms. The most important number to look at is the revenue per lawyer. Firms with high revenue per lawyer at least have the appearance of financial health, although, as we shall see later, they can still be on the verge of liquidation.

Second, although it is risky to rely on this attribute alone, firms that pay well generally do better financially for a variety of reasons. Such firms have the financial confidence to offer big bucks. That confidence reflects better clients and better work. Also, higher-paying firms can attract better lawyers. So recognize that an abnormally low salary range (judged by the standards of the peer group) may be indicative of some financial problems. Likewise watch out for firms that pay too well. There are always some "high flyers" that are about to crash and burn.

In evaluating pay, of course, it is not merely the starting salary that must be considered. It is important to consider the salary that is paid to associates as they progress in seniority. Such data is difficult to find, although most firms will not consider it impertinent to inquire at least in generalities about the topic.

Third, do an Internet search on the firm. Http://www.abovethelaw.com and other sites may give you some information about a firm's apparent financial condition. If you can—and in the current environment it may be hard—avoid firms that have laid off lawyers, rescinded offers, or told new associates to start their employment more than six months later than originally promised.[6] These actions are signs of financial declines that you want to avoid, if you can. Also be careful about firms that do not make offers to virtually all of their summer associates. This

---

6. In my view, it is preferable to work for a firm that has, at least initially, cut back salaries rather than attorneys. The firm that cuts attorneys as a first response to economic stress is demonstrating a far more callous manner of dealing with attorneys. Cutting salaries is a way of spreading the pain more evenly.

decision is also a sign of financial stress.

In my view, it is not useful in most cases to raise issues of firm finances during your interview with the firm. It will immediately put the interviewer on the defensive, and you will rarely get an honest answer. Who needs associates—much less applicants—who ask too many sensitive questions?

Although financial issues have recently dominated the conversation about firms, there are other issues to consider as well. Does the firm have a good reputation as a place to work, or is it a "dog eat dog" world rife with infighting? Does the firm worship the billable hour and dump you in the library to be forgotten by everyone except the computer that spits out monthly bills, or does it offer a good platform for your further development as a lawyer? Does it contribute, and allow you to contribute, to the community through pro bono legal work or otherwise? Is it a diverse place, or is the firm socially homogenous? Does it try to promote its associates to partnership or does it expect you to leave after a few years? Nowadays you may not have as much opportunity to be selective, but these issues are all important to consider if you have more than one opportunity to pursue.

In choosing firms, it is always worth considering the benefits of a large firm versus a small firm. For me, any firm with fewer than one hundred lawyers is a small firm. Any firm with over one thousand lawyers is a "megafirm." Between one hundred and one thousand lawyers is what I would call "large." There is no easy way to compare these apples, but one can make some crude observations.

Smaller firms generally tend to offer more responsibility to younger lawyers but have fewer resources for training them. Smaller firms value their investment in associates and tend to want to make them partners. Megafirms tend to look at lawyers as commodities, although they often get the most interesting cases. Smaller firms require better interpersonal skills. Larger firms are more tolerant of bright specialists who have weaker interpersonal skills. But these generalizations always have exceptions. Look carefully at each firm. If you have a choice, find the one in which you will feel most at home.

A special word for women and minority applicants is in order. In choosing firms, try to find firms that already have a substantial group of women and minority lawyers. It is very isolating to be a lone pioneer, even though the firm may be well intentioned in hiring you. And at a moment when you are just getting familiar with legal practice, you do not want to have an additional job challenge.

Government Jobs

If you can find a good job in government, there is nothing more rewarding than serving your community. There is great opportunity in the government to obtain responsibility and experience early in your career. The disadvantages are that training is usually less rigorous, caseloads are generally excessive, and the quality of the work suffers. You can pick up a lot of bad habits from overworked and underpaid lawyers. Additionally, unless you make it a career, government service does not equip you well to function in a capitalist world. Since, as a government lawyer, you have captive clients, you do not have the incentives to develop marketing skills to the degree you would in private life. Put another way: when you have a paycheck that is guaranteed, you do not have the motivation to develop your business contacts.

There are a wide variety of possible jobs in the state and federal governments well suited for new lawyers. Of course, you can work as a criminal prosecutor or a public defender. But in addition, you can work for a large variety of agencies. The list is as endless as the seemingly boundless scope of government in our society.

If community service appeals to you, you should get some advice on which agencies provide the best training and experience. Be as discriminating as you can. Getting the job may involve some politics, so ask your law school or alumni of the school for some insight into the process so that you will not waste time on unproductive applications. Here networking is often the key to success.

Once again, please keep in mind the need for being geographically nimble in today's market. There are often jobs in government agencies in remote parts of the United States, which can give you good experience and ultimately lead to other jobs in similar agencies in other parts of the country. For example, you could start with a federal agency in a remote area, where competition is less, and later move to an office of that agency in a more desirable location. Or you could start as a prosecutor in a rural area and use the experience to move to an urban area. The fewer limitations you set on your first job search, the more likely it will be that you will get a job in a difficult economic period.

In-House Counsel Jobs

Though the bulk of new law graduates enter the profession through other routes, every year a substantial percentage of law graduates go to work in corporate law departments. It is worth taking a moment to point out the tremendous opportunities that exist "in-house," as well as the challenges that exist in the corporate world.

Corporate law firms are generally small. Most companies cannot afford to have giant law firms in-house or do not see the need for them. If you like the sheer joy of American entre-preneurial capitalism, however, I can think of no better place to work. You can be both a lawyer and a client. You can be a businessperson as well as an attorney. You can offer creative solutions to minimize legal risk to the business in a wide variety of areas. You don't have to search for clients; you search for good outside counsel. Often you are not expected to work more than 9:00–5:00. While attorneys in law firms are working until 3:00 a.m. to get a brief out, you are at home sleeping.

For a new lawyer in a corporation, the reality may be a little less romantic, of course. But for my money, in-house lawyers participate in one of the most creative and enjoyable walks of life. They don't have to worry about billable hours. They have to focus entirely on client service. They get to learn many aspects of law. In good companies, they are called upon for advice that is honored by everyone in the company.

There are, of course, some drawbacks. Corporate law departments are small groups that place a high value on interpersonal and communications skills. Training is often on-the-job simply because the elaborate training that is often available in the government and in large law firms is not available. You will generally be called upon to give a lot of accurate advice quickly and will have to become a good counselor to your business colleagues. As an in-house attorney, you are expected to "add value." Of course, when you try to explain how you are adding value by approving the invoices of outside counsel, you may receive some skeptical, if not sarcastic, comments from businesspeople who think that lawyers are an impediment to everything productive in life.

As an associate in a large law firm or a lawyer in government, you are not in charge of the budget. But in all corporations, the budget is critical to everyone—and to their bonuses! Even though you are not in control of all of the legal crises that occur in the life of the corporation, the company will demand that you move heaven and earth to control costs. The budget always produces high stress for in-house counsel. Money is not endless; companies are driven to achieve their quarterly and annual earnings estimates.

One drawback of starting in-house is that you may have relatively few opportunities to advance in the organization. Few businesses focus on promoting lawyers. They want to promote businesspeople rather than create a large in-house law firm with a hierarchy of lawyers. Also, starting in-house may tend to foreclose options to go to work for a firm at a later point. My experience has been that making the transition from an in-house role to a firm role is not easy. In-house, you often have the option of delegating the detailed legal work to outside counsel. That is not necessarily the best preparation for firm life.

Teaching

Although I come from a family steeped in academic life, I have chosen not to be a permanent academic. That said, it has always seemed to me that teaching is the highest calling in a civilized society. It gives you an unparalleled opportunity to make a real difference in the lives of your students and the many clients and communities they will serve. If you like research and writing, you will have ample time to do it in depth. So if you have the opportunity to teach, it is well worth pursuing it.

There are drawbacks to teaching. Jobs are scarce. Generally schools will not look at you unless you had stellar grades. Additionally, clerkships and/or stints in a government agency are valued credentials.

In my mind, however, the worst drawback to teaching is the tremendous infighting that generally goes on at academic institutions. Not only do you have the pressure to do research and to publish, but you also have to deal with academic committees, contentious faculty, and, sometimes, contentious students. You are in the public light continuously and have to act as though your every word were being transcribed.

You will generally make less money than your colleagues in the legal profession, even though your status may be higher by far. You may have to endure a lot of criticism of your work, even if it is good. And you will generally be doomed to lecture on the same material year after year until you either hate it or fall passionately in love with it.

It is also worth keeping in mind that there are often opportunities for part-time teaching as an adjunct professor. In this way, you can have a career in private practice and still participate in the intellectual life of a law school without some of its hassles.

Working as a Contract Attorney

In recent years, there has been a proliferation of agencies that rent lawyers on a contract basis to law firms with excess capacity. Working as a contract attorney involves short-term stints in firms needing lawyers to do document review and menial work. The advantage for the law firm is that it makes no commitment to the contract attorney and provides no benefits. The advantage for the contract attorney is that there is work and a paycheck to put food on the table.

I do not judge the process, since it is a market phenomenon, but it has always seemed to me that working as a contract attorney is one of the last resorts. If there is no commitment on either side of the relationship and the work is menial, how can this employment benefit a new lawyer? Where can the new attorney gain experience? Where is the training that is so important early in the new lawyer's career? And most importantly, where is the personal commitment of the firm to the new attorney?

THE MECHANICS OF JOB HUNTING

At the outset, let me say that getting a job is a lot like speed dating. There is a very limited amount of time in which the interviewer has to make a decision from among various candidates. In this process, unfortunately, initial impressions count for a lot, and preconceptions abound. Try to show that your abilities and interests fit the job description, that you are great person, and that you are willing to invest in the organization for the long haul. To do this, you have principally two tools: the resume and the interview.

Preparing a Resume

Much has been written about the perfect resume. Most of the resumes I see are well constructed; law schools and colleges appear to teach resume writing quite well. Basically, a resume should be neat and easy to read. It should highlight the best points about the applicant, especially the ones that set the applicant apart from other applicants. It is equally important, however, that the resume be honest. Exaggerated claims about how you single-handedly tried a complex securities trial while working as a summer clerk for a law firm are likely to instantly disqualify you. Likewise, do not attempt to "enhance" your academic credentials by rounding up your class rank or grade point average. This exaggeration will be viewed as cheating.

When reviewing a resume, employers principally look at four things: First, they want to see that you have sufficient ability to handle the demands of the practice. This is often a review of your academic credentials, but special skills, such as foreign language ability, are also relevant. Second, they want to see a record of proven performance. They want to know that they can rely on you to work hard and productively. They are interested in the awards and other successes noted on your resume. Third, employers want to see that you have a genuine interest in the type of work in which the organization is engaged. For example, if you are going to work for a corporate law firm, your undergraduate degree in accounting might be helpful. Fourth, employers are interested in knowing something about your relevant personal interests without asking questions that would be inappropriate or illegal. Community involvement is a perfect example of relevant and important information. Marital and health status are not.

Lawyers with experience should include historical information about the types of cases or transactions they have handled, the degree of responsibility they have been assigned, their billable hours, fee receipts (i.e., money received from their own labor), and the amount of business they have produced and can bring with them. Such information goes to the heart of the "economic question" and helps a prospective employer focus on other important aspects of the candidate's credentials.[7]

Let me say a word about listing references in your resume. References are helpful to the degree that (a) the reference really knows the applicant, (b) the reference is prepared to respond positively to inquiries, and (c) the reference is honest. Frequently, however, I have found that the reference is not expecting a call

---

7. If you are a more senior attorney and have no business, you should prepare a detailed business plan that outlines your marketing strategy going forward. I will have a lot more to say about this in the chapter on marketing.

because the candidate has not asked for permission to list the reference. Other times the reference is so glowing that it is more of a sales pitch (perhaps by an existing employer who wants to unburden him or herself of the candidate). And often the reference has little or no real experience with the candidate's work and is not competent to render an informed opinion. So exercise care when picking and listing references.[8] If you are not certain of the value of a reference, don't list the person. Alternatively, you can simply wait until you are asked for references; you may not be asked.

Finally, be aware that employers increasingly use the Internet to check candidates. Some childish nonsense you put on your Facebook profile page or other Internet sites could undermine your resume. It is always a good idea to Google your own name to see what comes up and take appropriate measures to limit damage from any erroneous impressions. Indeed, you can actually use social networking sites to enhance your job search by posting your resume and other relevant information.

Writing Samples

Generally you should include a writing sample with your resume or at least offer to provide one. Later in this book, we will spend some time on legal writing. Please read it before you submit your writing sample. In choosing a sample, try to find one that has been reviewed by a professor and determined to be satisfactory. Polish it as you would a fine piece of furniture.

---

8.   Ideally, in the course of your law school career, you will have gotten to know professors or lawyers by working for them. These contacts will be great resources when it comes to references.

Interviews

Resumes are obviously critical to opening a conversation with employers. Interviews are, in varying degrees, critical to sealing the deal. The importance of interviews varies considerably depending on the circumstances. An on-campus interview, where the interviewer is trying to interview twenty candidates in a day, can be critical. If you don't stand out in the interviewer's mind at the end of the day, you will not be asked back to the firm for further interviews. Often this is a matter of your placement in the schedule. The first and last interviewees tend to stand out.

Interviews count for a lot more in smaller organizations than in larger ones. If, for example, you are applying for a job as the sole associate in a three-lawyer firm, you can bet that the interviewers will want to see if you are personally compatible. Large organizations can tolerate mistakes more easily, and the interview will count for less than the resume.

A lot has been written on interview techniques. Most of it is interesting, but not all that helpful. Here are a few ideas I have found over the years that will markedly improve your performance.

Bring extra copies of your resume and writing sample. Interviewers lose these things because they are disorganized, distracted, and distressed. By helping them cope with this situation, you will make them feel organized, focused, and calm. Not only will this make you more appealing to them, but it is, after all, the job of a new lawyer.

When interviewing, dress conservatively. You want to establish that you are going to fit into the organization. Because you cannot know exactly what the people in the firm wear, choose something that will not be the focus of the interview. Men should preferably wear a dark suit, white shirt, and a conservatively striped tie. Women should wear a conservative suit.

In an interview, you want to show that you are enthusiastically aligned with the organization. Stand out as someone who will not only fit in well, but someone who will hit the ground running and continue to run for a long time.

I recommend that you spend time extensively studying the firm or organization with which you are interviewing and its lawyers before the interview. Most interviewers will recognize that you have taken some time to learn about their organization and will be impressed by it. You may also avoid putting your foot in your mouth by asking questions about subjects that are painful, like the firm's recent loss of a $300 million case.

In researching a firm, the things to look for are significant cases, transactions, and clients with which the firm has been involved. A lot of this information can be found in Web sites, blogs, newspapers, and journals, such as *The American Lawyer* and in reported cases. The *Martindale Hubbell Directory* is also a valuable source of information and is available online. A Lexis/Nexis or Westlaw search may also uncover information about interesting cases in which the firm has been involved.

In the interview, stress your desire to work hard, to learn from the more experienced lawyers in the firm, to participate as a member of the team, and to eventually develop business for the firm. In a competitive world, it is a fact of life that these qualities will always make you valuable. Present your qualifications with humility but not excessive modesty. Sell yourself, at least a little bit. Silence in an interview is fatal; therefore, risk being a little too animated. You should have a few thirty-second "sound bites" to get your point across.

You may be asked if you want to work in the transactional practice or in litigation. This is a difficult question to answer. Nowadays jobs are so scarce that it makes sense to answer that you are open to opportunity in both areas and that you are still too young in the profession to have preconceived notions about one area or another. If, however, you are clearly committed to working in one area, it is wise to be honest. In any event, it is very difficult to know the area in which the firm is hiring. It may well be that despite the downturn it is looking for a transactional associate.

Since one of the goals of any interview is to show that you are special—and twenty minutes is very little time to do that—develop beforehand a list of things you want to present about yourself during the interview. For example, it might be helpful to point out that you worked in a legal aid office or worked on interesting cases that gave you some experience in litigation. Everyone has experiences that can be valuable preparation for the work. You want to be able to work them into your conversation in an unforced way.

Before going to the interview, try to picture yourself in your mind as positive, confident, self-assured, and articulate. Visualize a time and place when you were confident and successful, and then try to remember how you felt and acted. Practice walking and sitting in a confident and winning manner. I guarantee you these simple exercises will unconsciously help improve your performance. Also practice your interview; speak out loud. (I suggest a private location for this exercise.) If you can, use a mirror or a camcorder to look at yourself. Don't be afraid—this is a chance to pump yourself up.

It is wise to let the interviewer lead the interview, at least to start. But keep in mind that, to some degree, you want to get across your enthusiasm for the job possibility. Sitting passively while the interviewer lectures to you will not make you stand out—it will make you invisible.

It is impossible to predict all of the questions that may come up in an interview. Try to answer all appropriate and legal questions honestly. If you do not know an answer, say you don't know. If you face an illegal question (e.g., your marital status), it is best to deflect the question politely by answering in an oblique way that addresses the ultimate issue on which the interviewer is focused. For example, you might respond to a question about your marital status with the answer that you fully intend to remain in the community and to work hard to become a partner in the firm. If you don't need the job, you can be confrontational about an illegal question, but as I have learned the hard way, making enemies unnecessarily is not desirable.[9]

Many interviewers use "behavioral" or "situational" interviewing techniques. These interviewers will ask you a question aimed at seeing how you would react to situations. For example, an interviewer might say, "tell me about a time when you had too much work to do. How did you handle it?" Give a concrete example. You should be prepared to present clearly the situation you faced, the strategy you used to cope with it, and the results you obtained. Finally, relate the example to the work you anticipate facing in the firm and describe how your strategy would enable you to be effective in the firm.

To some degree, you can prepare for behavioral and situational questions. They all involve some stressful situation, like "a mistake you made and how you corrected it." For example,

---

9. You need, of course, to consider whether you want to work for a firm that asks illegal questions. However, the mistake of one lawyer may not be dispositive of the question. You have to see what the firm as a whole is like.

as an interviewer myself, I have sometimes presented a hypo-
thetical situation in which a client calls up an associate and
complains about the quality of the work and the fact that a motion was lost. I then ask candidates what they would do in this
situation. You would do well to prepare cogent descriptions of
situations where you handled the stress of interpersonal and
professional problems with skill, organization, and, ultimately,
success.

Let the interviewer lead the questioning, but don't be afraid
to ask your own questions. Avoid arguments. Successfully debating your interviewer might land you a job, but it is more
likely it will not.

During the interview, here are five questions you can always
ask without fear of embarrassment:

1. Will you please tell me about your practice?
2. What kind of lawyers do you like to hire?
3. Can you tell me about how associates are assigned?
4. Can you tell me why you like the firm?
5. How long does it typically take to become a partner?

Here are the top four questions to avoid:

1. What is your minimum billable hour requirement?
(Sounds like you want to shoot for the minimum.)

2. How much vacation will I get? (Forget it. They never
want you to go on vacation, particularly when you have not
even started work.)

3. Do you expect me to work nights and weekends? (Ask
a dumb question and you will get a dumb answer.)

4. What does your firm do to promote healthy lifestyles?
(Translation by interviewer: I want to goof off.)

It is helpful to make some notes about each interview
right after you leave the firm and then send a short note to each

interviewer thanking him or her for taking time to speak with you. You can also tell each one how much you enjoyed talking about whatever you discussed. It is good to remember that decisions about offers are sometimes made after the day of the interview, and you can improve your chances of being remembered favorably by writing a note.

THE BAR BLUES

You may not need to pass the bar examination and the accompanying character investigation to get a job, but you will almost certainly need to pass in order to keep a job as a lawyer. Whatever the theoretical merits of the bar admission process may be, it is a required rite of passage. Moreover, passing the bar substantially enhances your marketability as a lawyer.

Bar review courses are extremely good at teaching you how to pass the bar. I only have a few short thoughts to add.

The bar examination is a trauma because so much rides on the outcome. There is no sugar coating a difficult process in which you will be filling out extensive and intrusive questionnaires, studying for weeks, and waiting in suspense for months. That said, for those who accept the process and study hard, bar admission is easier than for those who resist. If you are positively motivated, the bar review courses can be an opportunity to listen to good lecturers give you an overview of law and to teach you some new material that might be of interest.

The good news—if you can call it that—is that the test is pass/fail and nobody will ever know or care about your grade once you pass the examination. The eventual pass rate for the bar examination is reasonably high in most states.[10] You can

10.   *See,* statistics available at the website of the National Conference of Bar Examiners, http://www.ncbex.org/bar-admissions/stats/.

take it more than once. So relax and make the best of it. You may never fully master the Rule Against Perpetuities or understand why you were tested on it. But you will become a lawyer at the end of the process.

In my experience, a great many of those who cannot pass the bar examination fall into three groups: (a) those that do not study, (b) those whose first language is not English, and (c) those who are totally freaked out by the examination. In most cases these are curable conditions. In the cases in which it is not, I can only suggest that you seek a state with a higher pass rate. After a few years, you can move around more freely by "waiving into" other states.

Finally, when responding to the character investigation, be scrupulously honest and blunt. Most of the transgressions of your youth can be excused if they are revealed honestly. Lying is not an option in this or any other aspect of legal practice.

WHAT IF YOU CAN'T FIND A JOB?

What happens if you cannot find a job? Don't give up. Be disciplined and creative. First, decide why you have not found a job. In my experience, there are really only two groups of new lawyers without jobs. The first group consists of market casualties. The market is bad; their grades are low; their school is not held in high esteem; and employers are afraid to hire them. Or they are too inflexible in their own job demands for the market to accommodate them. The second group includes, but is not limited to, lawyers who don't know why they want to be lawyers. Their schools may have failed to motivate them. Perhaps their circumstances do not motivate them enough to push through the last barriers to becoming lawyers. They keep thinking they would like to do something else.[11]

To both groups I have the same answer: I want you in my profession! I am not prepared to give up on you. You have worked hard for your degree. Before you give up on three years of education, you ought to have the opportunity to practice law. There will be plenty of time to give up on being a lawyer later, *after* you have had a chance to experience the profession. I don't want it to end now. And, deep down, neither do you.

How about volunteering to work in legal aid, a court, or governmental agency for a while? It may be hard for you to get a paying job in the public sector, but there are many opportunities for volunteers in many agencies. The experience will make you more marketable and lead to a paying job within a reasonable time. If your finances do not permit you to work full time for free, maybe you can work part of the time in an unpaid job as a lawyer and part of the time in a paying job related to the law (e.g., Westlaw representative). Remember, your underemployment is only a short-term issue. You will find a job, particularly if you analyze the market and stay flexible.

What about working as a paralegal? Firms are often looking for paralegals, and your credentials as a lawyer will make you exceptionally valuable. In contrast to working as a contract lawyer, working as a paralegal makes you part of the team. The firm will have made some commitment to you and will take pride in your accomplishments. Once you are in the firm and can prove your worth, you may have the inside track for associate openings. You will know the firm, the people, and the work.

---

11. There is a small third group: those with mental illness or drug abuse. Obviously if you are in this group, please get professional treatment. Your family and your community need you.

If you are good, you will have a good shot at the job. So suck in your pride, take a status cut, get some solid experience, and make yourself known in a firm you respect.

The value of networking can never be overestimated. Be sure to join bar associations and other organizations where you can network. You will learn of jobs informally through networking. When I say "join," I mean really join in. Make an effort to participate in the work of the organization. You will meet a lot of lawyers that way who will come to know your worth. Networking is not a superficial exercise; it requires getting to know people in a reasonably close way.

Another possibility is to hang out your shingle and become a solo practitioner. Having spent many years as a solo, I can tell you that it is a difficult road to travel, even for an experienced lawyer. For a new lawyer, it is fraught with peril. Not only can it be very lonely, but you will also have few mentors to offer the on-the-job training so essential for a new lawyer. Economically, there is also a much greater risk. You must make a significant investment of capital and time. Unless you are one of the very few that can develop a boutique niche practice in a short time, you will have to become a jack-of-all-trades and take on whatever types of clients and work come in without much selectivity. It is a recipe for trouble.

If you are still determined to become a solo practitioner, I recommend reading Jay Foonberg's book *How to Start and Build a Law Practice* (5th Ed.), published by the American Bar Association. It is an encyclopedia of everything you need to know about the nuts and bolts of building a solo law practice. I also recommend it to everyone else for its common-sense answers to the many practical questions that arise in any practice.

Remember, the most important rule of starting out in a solo practice is to ask experienced attorneys for advice. It is generally free and, unlike many things in life, worth more than you pay for it. It is also a good source of networking referrals. Solos always like to refer other solos, if it is appropriate. And you may find valuable opportunities to collaborate with more experienced attorneys in handling cases.

As a last resort, some attorneys choose to go back to school to acquire an LLM degree. There are many fine programs available. For specialties such as taxation, it is highly advantageous to have the degree. However, my own view is that for most people, pursuing another degree will run up expense for which there will be no certainty of reward. It also may divert your attention from the work of finding a job.

The history of the legal profession has shown that lawyers rarely get rich, but they do not starve. Today's market is challenging, but the world has not changed that profoundly for lawyers. If you stay positive and harness that positive energy, you will get your first job. I hope, too, that as you endure its anxieties you can also enjoy the adventure of the process.

THE FIRST DAY

Your first day on any job is very important. Consciously and unconsciously people remember their first impression of you. Apart from being well dressed and well groomed (in accordance with the codes of the firm), there are a number of things you should do.

Try to introduce yourself to as many people as you can. "Hi, I'm John Smith, a new associate in the litigation department. Who are you? What do you do here?" Shake people's hands. You are now a politician, and politicians like to shake hands and remember names. (At least you do not have to kiss babies!) If you have a hard time remembering the names, try to repeat the name back to the person ("How do you do, Ms. Wilson?").

Be interested in everyone, including non-lawyers. Non-lawyers are employees just like you, with one exception. Virtually any member of the non-legal staff may become crucial to the performance of any lawyer, now or at some future point of time. Being able to mobilize non-lawyers to accomplish the impossible under great stress will make you a hero. By the same token, your inability to mobilize them will diminish your value and may even spell disaster.

In most firms, you will be introduced to a great number of people. I recommend that you try to ask each one of them something about themselves and try to write it down unobtrusively so that you can recall it later. Good politicians never forget a face or a name and some fact about the person. It is an acquired talent. I once asked a famous politician who introduced himself to me at a party how he knew my name and what my father had done for a living. He winked and pulled out a little card he had in his pocket with the names of all of the people he wanted to meet at the party with a brief note on each one. So use this tried and true political trick, and you will be ahead of the game.

On your first day, it is vital that you learn where everything is. Know where the library is located. If the books are spread out in the firm, try to spot where they are. Find out where the mailroom is. Ask where the copiers are located. Law firms are communications nerve centers. Carefully learn the e-mail and word-processing systems so that you can prepare documents and send and receive e-mail. Learn to operate telephones, including any features that permit conference calling, transfer of calls, and speed dialing.

Part of your first day (or days) should also be devoted to learning the full computer capabilities of your firm. Often there is software available to you that does not generally get distributed.[12] You should find software that will track your contacts and keep your schedule. These are two essential facets of the work of a lawyer. Not only is it necessary to find telephone

---

12.   This would include practice specific software such as Summation and Case Map, which are used for litigation management.

numbers and e-mail addresses quickly, but it is also necessary to keep track of the network of attorneys who can be sources of referrals over the years. We will be talking about networking more fully later on.

I suggest that you take careful notes on your first day. There is a lot to absorb, and you want to have good recall. Somehow people have the strange notion that you should remember everything they told you on the first day. If you forget, ask again. If you have notes, you will ask fewer times.

LEGAL RESEARCH

Your first research assignments in a firm are very important. Like first impressions, they tend to mark you. In this section, I am going to give you some specific ideas that will guarantee that you will be seen as a good researcher, even if you were not at the top of your class in law school.

Please get over the idea that research is second-class work. That is ridiculous. Learning the law is essential to your legal career. The research you do contributes to your knowledge, while providing the foundation for the legal product of your firm. Your research can literally make or break a case. If you find a rule of law that permits a transaction to go forward on a tax-free basis, you may make the client very happy. Conversely, a mistake in your research can have a devastating impact. For example, suppose a litigator in your firm prepares a defense at trial based on your research, and then the opposing party files a motion to preclude the defense, predicated on a case you overlooked. It could not only be fatal to your colleague's case, but to your reputation at the firm as well.

In the firm where I was lucky to be an associate, research was seen as a primary tool that had to be mastered by all of the lawyers working together. The library had the best view in the office and plenty of space. It was not uncommon to see senior partners in the library checking references and researching legal issues. Sadly, there are firms today where research is not seen as an exalted intellectual art but as demeaning drudgery. Partners seem to think they should stay away from research because it is not "cost effective." The truth is quite the opposite. Experienced researchers can obtain relevant data so quickly that clients are often better served by having them perform the research, even at a higher hourly rate.

In any event, you should always take pride in your research. Understand that it is vitally important to your clients' cases and to your own development, as you expand your knowledge of the law and grow in the maturity of your judgments. It is also a way for you to improve your writing skills and, through the discipline of the written word, to perfect your legal analysis.

The first rule of good research is to make sure that you *understand the assignment clearly* and write it down. The more clearly you define the assignment, the more accurate and useful your research will be. Be sure that you question the assigning lawyer about all of the facts pertinent to the research inquiry. A small change in the facts can make a big difference in any conclusion you may reach. Ask specifically how much time the assigning lawyer thinks you should spend on the task, as well as the date and time it is due. Ask whether the assigning lawyer wants you to write a memorandum on your research and what format should be used to write the memorandum.

Be sure that your research is thorough. The most common mistake new lawyers make is to find something that appears to answer the assigned question and then stop researching. In so doing, they miss subsequent opinions granting rehearing and withdrawing the initial opinion. They miss appellate cases reversing the case on which they have relied. They miss subsequent cases that have overturned the rule or even a whole line of cases that are contrary to the initial rule they found. They miss the opinion written by the judge, before whom the firm's case is pending, severely criticizing the rule and distinguishing the precedent upon which they rely on its facts. They miss law review articles explaining the precedent or arguing for a change in the precedent. They miss the fact that there is a case pending before the state supreme court in which the rule is being challenged. I can attest to the potential for these oversights because I have personally made, or witnessed, all of these mistakes.

In order to avoid these and other similar disasters, *begin the research manually.* Do not use computer aids until you have gained a mastery of the issue from traditional methods. Computers tend to limit your focus, because they are mindlessly dependent on the quality of the query. At the outset of the research, expand your focus to avoid missing any issue. Try to find a law review article or treatise covering the issues. Someone spent hours and hours researching the area to prepare the article or treatise. Use these tools as a starting point, and you will be way ahead in surfacing the law and understanding the issues.

After you have manually researched the issue, then follow out the subsequent history of every case and every relevant head-note or key number by computer. If there is no controlling authority, search other jurisdictions. Look at the statutes to see if there is a statutory rule that has changed the case law. Follow the statutes to and including the latest session of the legislature. Look for legislative history. Try to find out if there is anything pending in any appellate court that might be of interest, including briefs on appeal.

All new lawyers are familiar with Westlaw and Lexis because they have been provided free in law school to hook law students. In using computerized research, however, you can also use the Internet to supplement these expensive services at no charge to your clients. Most appellate courts have opinions available for free on Web sites. Many appellate courts provide access to briefs and oral arguments online. And many of the trial courts are moving to systems that allow computer access to orders and other unpublished documents in the files that can be very helpful.

You may want to recommend that your firm subscribe to Loislaw, Fastcase, and Heinonline. Loislaw and Fastcase are less expensive computer research tools that are almost as good as Westlaw. Heinonline is an inexpensive service providing unlimited access to a wide variety of law review articles.

Writing a memorandum summarizing your research is critical. Even if it is not part of the assignment, I recommend writing a memorandum to record your research. In the course of a year, you will work on so many matters that without a memorandum, you will not be able to remember your research should you be called upon to revisit the issues. In the next chapter, we will come back to the style of the memorandum, but for now, suffice it to say that the memorandum is essential. Remember, a good lawyer always has a memorandum.

WRITING MEMORANDA, LETTERS, PLEADINGS, AND CORPORATE DOCUMENTS

GENERAL TIPS FOR IMPROVING YOUR WRITING STYLE

The best legal writing is concise, but, alas, most legal writing is verbose. In this chapter, I will give you a lot of advice about writing, but none more important than this:

Please keep it as short and as clear as possible. Avoid pretentious legal jargon. Write so that even a non-lawyer can understand your message.

Know the objective of your writing. Is your document an objective analysis? Or is it intended to persuade? Is the tone as informal as a quick memo between colleagues? Or is it as formal as the Declaration of Independence?

Assume that the reader has a short attention span and needs to obtain information quickly. Avoid long sentences, complicated paragraphs, and words with no discernible meaning. If you want a good model, carefully written by a great writer and lawyer, read and reread Lincoln's Gettysburg Address. Only two minutes long, it far eclipsed the lofty two-hour oration of Edward Everett, which preceded it. For ease of reference, here it is:

Four score and seven years ago our fathers brought forth on this continent a new nation, conceived in Liberty, and dedicated to the proposition that all men are created equal.

Now we are engaged in a great civil war, testing whether that nation, or any nation, so conceived and so dedicated, can long endure. We are met on a great battle-field of that war. We have come to dedicate a portion of that field, as a final resting place for those who here gave their lives that that nation might live. It is altogether fitting and proper that we should do this.

But, in a larger sense, we can not dedicate—we can not consecrate—we can not hallow—this ground. The brave men, living and dead, who struggled here, have consecrated it, far above our poor power to add or detract. The world will little note, nor long remember what we say here, but it can never forget what they did here. It is for us the living, rather, to be dedicated here to the unfinished work which they who fought here have thus far so nobly advanced. It is rather for us to be here dedicated to the great task remaining before us—that from these honored dead we take increased devotion to that cause for which they gave the last full measure of devotion—that we here highly resolve that these dead shall not have died in vain—that this nation, under God, shall have a new birth of freedom—and that government: of the people, by the people, for the people, shall not perish from the earth.

Notice how tightly Lincoln organizes the address. He begins with a brief historical background for his speech, which was the original philosophical basis of the Union. He next presents the current background, the engagement of the nation in a civil war, and the need to dedicate a cemetery on a battlefield of the war. Next he presents the core of this argument, which is that we cannot dedicate the land better than those who fought on it. And finally he balances it all by presenting things that we can concretely do in the future, which are to take "increased devotion" to the original cause for which those who perished fought, to create a "new birth of freedom," and to save the Union.

The language of the address is clear and very succinct. With perhaps the exception of the first line's reference to "four score and seven," the language is plain. We can hear the beautiful cadence of each phrase building carefully and deliberately to the memorable final line.

The care with which the address was written and the methodical way in which Lincoln crafted his argument are the epitome of what we do as advocates. We can see why Lincoln was such a renowned lawyer. And while we will never duplicate his rhetoric and style, Lincoln's address is a wonderful model to keep in mind as we talk about legal writing.

As Lincoln most certainly did before writing the Gettysburg address, you have to think before you write. If your thinking is bad, your writing will be awful. Like so many things in life, good legal writing begins and ends with thoughtful organization. Think about the purpose of what you are writing and the audience to whom you are speaking.[13]

As you write—whether by keyboard or by dictation—listen to what you are saying. Hear the prose. When Lincoln wrote the Gettysburg Address, he obviously heard what he was going to say. In polishing the product, he focused on the cadence, the melody of the sentences. Although the audience that ultimately heard the speech was slow to embrace Lincoln's oral presentation, the address is remarkable as a piece of writing because of its melodic phrasing when read aloud. Few of us are likely to achieve such a poetic writing style, and time does not allow us the luxury of rewriting legal memoranda for weeks. But with a little effort, you can dramatically improve the quality of your writing.

Writing style is important and can be learned. I suggest that you begin by reading Strunk and White's short book *The*

---

13. Interestingly, although Lincoln's address received a chilly reception by the live audience on the battlefield, it received far more glorious reviews in the print media. Lincoln knew at the time he wrote the speech that most of his audience would never hear the speech but would read it in the newspapers. He wanted above all to make it readable and memorable.

Elements of Style. An early version of it is now available free online at http://www.bartleby.com/141/. It contains all the basic rules of usage and punctuation. If you follow these rules, you will not go wrong.

Sentence structure is vital. Here are four quick tips to boost the quality of your work:

1. Avoid fragments by always checking to be sure that each sentence has a subject and a verb that agree in both number and tense.

2. Eliminate run-on sentences or sentences that are too long to comfortably read. All sentences longer than two lines are suspect.

3. Correct dangling prepositions. (e.g., "That is the cause he pointed to." The correct version of this sentence is: "That is the cause to which he pointed.") Getting rid of dangling prepositions will markedly, and almost effortlessly, increase the quality of your written work.[14]

4. Use double dashes (known among editors as an "em dash" because it is the width of the letter "m") to insert parenthetical material and emphasize points. (e.g., "It is obvious—and I want to underscore this point—that typographical errors cannot be tolerated in a civilized world!")

Give careful thought to your paragraphs. They serve two purposes. First, they divide ideas, which improves organization. Second, they break up the manuscript so that it is easier to read. Disciplined thought and good aesthetics make written work easier to read and assimilate. When you consider where to divide paragraphs, keep this in mind.

---

14. The dangling preposition rule does, of course, have exceptions, as Winston Churchill famously pointed out, when he facetiously remarked, "That is an indignity up with which I will not put!"

Generally it is wise to begin the paragraph with a short sentence, which can act as an index tab for readers, particularly those who read quickly. If possible, have the sentence introduce the topic of the paragraph. Use varied sentence structure in the course of the paragraph to make the reading more interesting. However, avoid lengthy, convoluted, or run-on sentences,[15] which make reading the paragraph an exercise in endurance. Be certain to keep the tenses of verbs consistent within the paragraph so the reader knows whether you are talking about the past, present, or future. Try to make your prose pithy, punchy, and polished. And if you can do it, end the paragraph on a high note.

Punctuation is important. It helps the reader understand your intended meaning. Use *Elements of Style* to learn the rules. Remember that good writers often violate the rules, but they do so only for a conscious reason.

Use headings liberally to divide your paragraphs by subject matter. Remember, readers under time pressure sometimes need visual aids to comprehend where they are in a memorandum. They may read for a few minutes and pick up the rest later. Headings, like traffic signals, prevent accidents.

Finally, make your entire written work look professional. If it does not look like a professional wrote it, nobody will think you are a professional. And, oh, by the way, please proofread again and again and again.

USING DICTATION

What I am going to say now flies flatly in the face of everything you believe, but despite the countless hours we all spend

---

15. A run-on sentence is one that is grammatically incorrect. For example, "I went to the market I found no fish was available." Convoluted sentences, however, may be grammatically correct, but run on and on and on.

at computer keyboards, it is the truth. Dictation is a dramatically better way to write than typing. My father was an accomplished professional writer with a typing speed of about one hundred words per minute on an old manual typewriter (his typing sounded like machine gun fire). But he almost always began his first drafts by dictating.

My father knew that he could get the bulk of his work on paper at about 100-150 words per minute by dictating, without repetitive motion injury. He then could tinker with the document in any way he wanted. He also knew that by dictating he could improve the cadence of his writing—because he was listening to it.

Even given the fact that new lawyers today are generally proficient typists, most still only type at a rate of sixty words per minute. And when composing at the keyboard, they probably type no more than twenty-five words per minute. If you can raise your speed to 125 words per minute by dictating, you can improve your efficiency by 500 percent.

There is, unfortunately, an important caveat to all this talk of dictation: Not every law firm these days provides support for dictation. Still, many firms have secretaries and/or voice recognition software that can take a digital file and turn it into a document.

So why don't firms promote dictation? First of all, most partners don't dictate. Some even write out their work longhand. Sadly, in the billable hour world, there may even be unconscious financial reasons to be less efficient. But efficiency is important for clients. It is also important for new lawyers, whose productivity is a concern given the salaries they are paid. If you can improve your efficiency dramatically, you will be the "go to" associate for the best work. Believe me, inefficient associates are ultimately a plague to partners. It may be tolerated in brand new lawyers, but inefficiency is fatal for midlevel and senior associates.

At present, computer dictation programs, such as Dragon Naturally Speaking and Via Voice, are widely available. These programs translate your voice into a typed document. Unfortunately, these programs have never been used extensively in law firms for two reasons. First, the earlier versions of these computer programs required several months of training, during which time the program learned to read your voice intonation. Few lawyers have been inclined to spend the time. Second, the programs utilize a lot of computer RAM and file storage capacity. In large firms, this can be costly.

I am pleased to report that while RAM and storage issues continue, the very latest version of Dragon Naturally Speaking, Version 10.1 (currently available only from Nuance, the manufacturer) achieves very high accuracy with only a few minutes of training. Since you are likely to be one of the first lawyers to utilize this program, your firm should be able to provide computers with the requisite hardware requirements.[16] You will be quite surprised at how much this program improves your efficiency.

---

16.   According to the manufacturer, the program theoretically requires an Intel Pentium 4 processor, only one gigabyte of RAM to run on Windows Vista, and only 512 kilobytes of L2 cache. I doubt this will work well, particularly if you are running multiple programs simultaneously. My own experience is based on hardware with four gigabytes of RAM and six megabytes of L2 cache. Upgrading RAM is not that difficult or expensive these days. You can install the RAM yourself. Try http://www.18004memory.com for good deals and installation instructions.

Dictation Technique

I encourage you to learn to dictate. Here are some basic rules to get you started. I guarantee that if you follow them, you will be an accomplished "dictator" in less than a month.

1. Close the door to your office. It will drive everyone crazy to listen to your dictation, particularly when you are first learning.

2. Use a portable dictation device since it will allow you to quote from materials spread around your office. I particularly like digital dictation devices that permit you to edit and insert material after you have dictated it. Since this is an essential tool, you should invest in getting a comfortable dictation device. Be certain that you always have fresh batteries, since recording quality falls, and transcription errors increase, if the batteries begin to wear out.

3. *Outline very carefully what you are going to dictate.* The most frequent problem I encounter with novice dictators is that they produce "stream of consciousness" essays that are poorly organized and reasoned.

4. Organize the materials from which you are going to quote. If they have been photocopied, use a highlighter to highlight the legal principles upon which you are going to rely and the material from which you are going to quote. It may be better to give the highlighted portions to the legal assistant who is going to transcribe your dictation because this leads to fewer transcription errors.

5. Dictate at a moderate speed and speak distinctly. Remember, a human being still has to decipher your dictation. Be sure to include punctuation and to spell unusual words or words that are not commonly used by lay people.

6. Try to dictate the entire memorandum on a single tape or file. This will help ensure that one typist produces the basic text with a uniform typing style.

7. When you are done with the tape or file, make sure it is properly marked so that it does not get lost. When you send it for transcription, set a reasonable deadline for the return of the work. Remember, unreasonable deadlines stress the system and increase errors. Whenever possible, set transcription deadlines well in advance of the final deadline you face. Even under the best of circumstances, first drafts sometimes come back in rough condition. You may need time to revise your draft.

Working with a Draft

When you get the draft back, you should not worry about the fact that it is rough. It is the starting point for your work. Now you will begin crafting the final product, a process in which you will improve the organization, content, and style of the final product. You will then work on eliminating typographical errors, convoluted sentences, and lengthy paragraphs. You will also probably add some citations and more quoted material. You can also reorganize the presentation. However, since you originally took time with the organization before you began dictating, this process should be less serious and time consuming.

If you want to use your word-processing skills, now is the time to use them (or perhaps in the next draft). I find that editing on the computer yourself can be accomplished almost as quickly as writing out the changes for your legal assistant. This, of course, is a matter of personal preference. If the memorandum is long, however, you should realize that your less-than-professional word-processing edits may insert problem codes, profiles, styles, themes, and formats into the computer file and require a great deal of repair later. So when in doubt, please get a little help from the professionals. You can stick to the law!

WRITING MEMORANDA

Organize

Once again, as I said in the section on dictation, organization is the key to success. Outline the points of your memorandum on paper or computer screen in some logical order, whether it is the most important points first, the foundational points first, or the chronologically important points first.

It is important to have carefully read the cases you are going to cite in the memorandum so that you understand the legal principles they enunciate and the slight nuances of language that are often critical in the cases. Analyze the procedural posture of every case and read the facts of the cases. Always try to understand the underlying equities and economic issues of the cases.

Structure

If the assigning lawyer has not given you a special structure for writing your memorandum, here is one I think works well (including the headings):

1. **Scope of Memorandum.** In this section, simply restate the assignment. For example, "You have asked me to research the question of whether truth is a defense to a defamation action brought against our client for having taken out an

ad in the *XYZ Herald* accusing the plaintiff of being a corrupt politician. Set forth below is an analysis of that issue."

Notice that by restating the assignment, you are giving the assigning attorney an opportunity to revise the assignment and to be certain that you understood the assignment. It also gives anyone who reads the memorandum later on an understanding of the context and possible limitations of your research. In this connection, you might also add a footnote summarizing the sources you examined so that if additional work is done, it will not be repetitive.

2. **Statement of Facts.** In this section, provide a thorough, unbiased statement of all of the facts you have been given. It will be helpful for two reasons. First, it will serve as a record of the facts upon which you can draw when drafting pleadings. Second, it will alert the assigning attorney to any error in your factual assumptions that might have had an effect on the outcome of the research. Good factual development is essential to every case, and the time you spend on the statement of facts will be highly profitable.

3. **Issues Presented.** In this section, list the legal questions you have researched. This list will enable the person who reads the memorandum to understand the scope of your research and the structure of the memorandum. It will also force you to distill the legal issues rather than tackle them in a stream-of-consciousness memorandum.

4. **Summary of Conclusions.** In this section, which should rarely be longer than a page, tell the reader the outcome of the research. This is not only helpful to a reader who has a lot to read, but it will also help the reader understand the rest of the memorandum more effectively.

5. **Discussion.** In this section, present your research in detail. Remember that the presentation should not be argu-

mentative, unless that is what was requested. It should present arguments on both sides of the issues so that the reader can reach her or his own conclusions.

You should liberally quote from the sources of the research so that the reader will gain confidence that what you are saying is indeed based upon the research you have done. Nothing is less helpful than a "string cite" without an explanation of the cited cases. Even if you do no more than summarize the holding of each case in parentheses, you will give the reader heightened confidence in the validity of your presentation. It is also helpful to integrate quotes from the cases into your prose.

Before writing a memorandum, you might do well to ask the assigning lawyer for a memorandum to use as an example of the type of work he or she likes. Do not be a slave to this model, but use it as a guideline. I suggest organizing the discussion issue by issue. Set forth the issue and then the general legal principle to be applied. Apply the principle to your facts and reach a conclusion. Although this type of presentation is less creative than many, it has the advantage of being comprehensible and useful.

Use short sentences. Nothing is more difficult for an overworked reader than a convoluted sentence, no matter how grammatically correct it may be. Avoid stating conclusions without giving reasons. When stating a conclusion, liberally use the word "because." This ensures that you have a good reason for your conclusions, and it helps the reader come to believe that you can be relied upon to have good reasons.

Polishing the Product

It is unwise to present a memorandum of law in a rough form. Don't let anyone take it from you until you are satisfied that it is the best work of which you are capable. I cannot emphasize it enough: proofread the memorandum over and over again so there are no typographical errors. Such errors advertise you as a careless lawyer. Partners and clients do not like to pay for such work. Typos are not your secretary's fault; they are yours. And you will unfortunately pay a high price for them.[17] Also please keep in mind that computer spell checking is just the beginning of your proofreading. The computer does not do well with legal terms, citations, or grammar.

Avoiding Being Argumentative

The most common flaw in the memoranda I see from new lawyers is that the documents are too argumentative. New lawyers have a tendency to seize on one answer and to drive it home single-mindedly. The truth is that there are usually two or more sides to be argued on every issue, and a memorandum that at least presents the opposing arguments is a far more useful piece of work than one that obscures or underemphasizes them.

Final Checking

Before turning in a memorandum, you should completely cite check it using computerized methods, if possible. Although I am a skeptic of overreliance on computers for research in general, I believe that computers do a better job than people when it comes to cite checking. Always carefully compare your quotes to

---

17. The most egregious typographical error of which I ever heard was contained in a complaint filed in a federal court. The case involved an alleged product defect in a power lawn mower. The complaint, however, kept referring to a defective "paramour." The judge took great pleasure in reading the complaint to the jury at the outset, much to the dismay of the plaintiff's counsel and the plaintiff. The lawyer had obviously dictated the complaint but had never taken the time to review the typed document.

the original text. You should also look at the subsequent history of every case. Be sure to use the latest *Bluebook* form of citation.[18]

DRAFTING PLEADINGS AND MEMORANDA FOR USE IN COURT

After you have written a memorandum, you may be asked to prepare a pleading or some other form of written advocacy for use in court. These documents will require a different approach. You will have to argue points in a cogent way. This does not mean that you will ignore opposing authority. Nothing could be worse than failing to cite and distinguish the cases (particularly in your own jurisdiction) that hurt your position. Your opponent will almost certainly cite the cases, and the court will lose confidence in your entire presentation. You must not only present your argument with supporting authorities, but you must carefully distinguish opposing authorities and rebut opposing arguments. Judges will spot the fact that you have honestly presented your authorities and will be disposed to give you the benefit of many doubts in the case.

Before beginning to draft a pleading, it is essential that you understand what is required mechanically. You should review all of the applicable rules, federal, state, and local (including the rules of individual judges). Look for examples of the type of pleading required. Some pleadings are supposed to be bare-bones. Some are supposed to be in the form of detailed memoranda of law and facts. In every case, know the required form of the pleading. Some courts will penalize you for failing to follow the rules by striking your pleading. Some courts will not. But all courts appreciate the lawyers who try to follow the rules.

18.   The Bluebook: A Uniform System of Citation (Columbia Law Review Ass'n et al. eds.,18th ed. 2005).

You present yourself as a real "player" when you demonstrate knowledge of the finer points of the game.

As the junior lawyer on the project, it is your responsibility to learn and apply all of the "nit-picking" rules. Do not expect a senior lawyer to know the rules or notice all of your mistakes. Unfortunately, senior lawyers have many cases to handle and need to rely on junior lawyers to craft products that meet technical requirements.[19]

When you draft a memorandum for a judge to read, spend some time thinking about your audience. The judge is usually over forty years old. The judge usually has a prodigious caseload and very little time for your memorandum or for your case. The judge will be reading your work quickly. You, therefore, have to produce a product that gets directly to the point, concisely and clearly summarizes the arguments, and then supports or rebuts them with concrete facts and legal authority. Long, intellectual histories of legal issues are generally of no value to trial courts. The judge needs to grasp the facts, apply the correct law, and move on to the next motion. So even if you think you need to present some legislative history or some general background on the law, do it very concisely and show its relevance right away.

Whether it is fashionable to admit it or not, most lawyers have historically gotten paid by the page. The more time spent writing, the greater the fee. This has resulted in an unconscious view that long products are better. And sometimes it may even be true. So what I am going to say here will be a bit iconoclastic:

---

19. It goes without saying that if you are unsure of the technical requirements, ask questions of people in the firm or clerks of the courts. You will find court clerks—even in the Supreme Court of the United States—to be extremely helpful with respect to technical issues.

Every memorandum of law for a trial court can be written in twenty pages or less, particularly if relevant documents are put into appendices. By forcing yourself to stay within a twenty-page limit—even if it is not imposed by a court rule—you will improve the intensity and effectiveness of your argument.[20]

Make sure that you have an introductory paragraph that succinctly states (a) the procedural posture of the case, (b) the issues before the court, and (c) the conclusions of the memorandum (e.g., "The defendants have moved for summary judgment arguing that the undisputed facts show that there is no evidence of damage. This memorandum is submitted in opposition and shows that there are numerous disputed issues of fact with respect to the damage element of the case.").

You should then provide a succinct statement of the relevant facts. This statement should be scrupulously honest. Any distortion here will severely undermine your credibility. Nevertheless, you should obviously highlight those facts most supportive of your legal argument. Each factual statement should have a reference to something in the record (an affidavit, testimony, or an exhibit) that supports the statement.

Next, you should argue the issues one at a time, setting forth (a) the issue (or the argument you are attempting to rebut), (b) the applicable legal principle and authorities, and (c) the application of those principles and authorities to the facts of your case. Use headings liberally to divide the memorandum and highlight your points. You should always have a section at the end of the memorandum entitled "Conclusion" that sets forth

---

20. Footnotes can be helpful by providing detail without requiring the reader to lose his or her train of thought when reading. But keep in mind that in many jurisdictions, footnotes must be treated as normal text when computing page limitations.

the precise relief you are requesting (e.g., "Based upon the foregoing, the motion for summary judgment should be denied.").

You may wish, depending upon the local practice, to have a table of contents and a table of authorities in the beginning. Such tables can now be generated by word processors with relative ease (but they may take some time to code, so be sure to allow enough of it). Also consider using a slightly larger type font such as 14 Times Roman on your document. Almost everyone over the age of forty has to use eyeglasses to read. You would be surprised at how much more effectively you will reach your audience if you just make the type a little larger.

Finally, let me say a word about forms of pleadings and corporate documents that float around law firms and the Internet. *Forms can be—and often are—fatal!* It is all well and good to start with something that someone else has researched and written, but all too often new lawyers use this as a substitute for research and thinking. The citations in a form pleading, for example, are often completely out of date. Assume that whatever form you have been given needs to be rewritten and carefully adapted to the circumstances of your case.

DRAFTING CORPORATE DOCUMENTS

Very frequently, new lawyers are pressed into service to draft corporate documents, such as contracts and corporate minutes. My own experience was that this was initially the most terrifying type of assignment. Most law schools give you virtually no training in drafting corporate documents. The jargon is usually unfamiliar, and the pressure to produce the work very quickly is high. Here are a few tips for when you are suddenly thrown into a corporate drafting situation:

1. Know who the parties are, whom you represent, and what your client understands the deal to be. For this, you need good information—preferably including a term sheet.

2. Use forms to help with basic drafting, but remember to find out how slanted the draftsmanship in these forms has been. Each deal is slightly different, so you cannot mechanically rely on boilerplate language. Read the boilerplate carefully and be prepared to tailor the product to your transaction. Know why provisions are included and what provisions have been excluded. As with litigation documents, forms may be helpful and represent a great deal of accumulated legal wisdom, but they are potentially deadly. This is particularly true of corporate boilerplate that has to be read with utmost care to ensure that the provisions are clear, pertinent, and consistent. Remember that boilerplate is usually the product of a lot of prior contracts. Almost by definition, it is not tailored to your deal.

3. Keep in mind that all deals have tax and accounting consequences. Some have regulatory consequences. You have to know what they are. Often slight drafting changes can result in significantly different financial outcomes. If you don't know what the issues are, get help from experts in the area. Similarly, words may be terms of art, which have specific interpretation in the case law.

4. Avoid typographical errors. Once they are inserted into a document, they may never be found in the mountain of fine print. Your job is to make sure there are no such errors. For example, in defining the "Sellers" in a transaction with multiple selling entities, you may have unwittingly omitted the entity holding the principal assets to be sold.

WRITING LETTERS

The letter is an essential tool in the skill set of every lawyer. The quality of your letters will be an important advertisement of your skills. Letters are often persuasive tools. At other times, they are used to memorialize agreements and conversations. Sometimes they bring good news. Sometimes they are used to threaten legal actions. Make sure your letters are sharp and that you use them wisely.

The art of writing good letters is hard to develop. You must think and outline before you write a letter. Think about the purpose of the letter. Are you transmitting a document? Are you documenting some action or inaction? Are you setting forth an agreement? Are you giving advice? If you don't know exactly why you are writing a letter, don't write it.

Letters should be as short as possible and well organized. A crisp opening sentence should clearly set forth the purpose of the letter. For example:

Dr. Gene Fletcher
Department of Astrology
University of Mars
Kalamazoo, MI
  Re: Jones v. Kramer, Case No. 01-1289-CIV

Dear Dr. Fletcher:

  I write to set forth the terms under which you have agreed to serve as an expert witness in a products liability case involving our client, Mr. Jones.

Notice that I have included a "Re" line to make certain that the case is identified. This will avoid confusion at many stages, including the stage at which your legal assistant files the letter.

The body of the letter should consist of paragraphs that deal concisely with the specific issues. It is often useful to use headings and to number the points for easy reference. If the letter is disorganized, it will serve no purpose.

The closing should ideally be as polite as possible. Use sentences such as these: "I look forward to hearing from you." "If you have any questions, please to do not hesitate to call." "If there is any question about these terms, please let me know immediately." These sentences are more than polite fluff. They may well establish an agreement by silence. Additionally, they may leave the reader in a better frame of mind and more likely to agree with your positions.

Keep your prose simple and use the active voice. For example, it is far more assertive to say, "My client wishes to conclude this matter promptly" than to say, "A prompt conclusion of this matter is desired by my client." In fact, the latter passive construction may even introduce doubt that the lawyer shares the client's motivation.

Keep the letters as short as possible given the circumstances. What you say can get you into more trouble than what you do not say. In writing lengthy letters, you may make damaging and unnecessary admissions, raise new and contentious issues, and complicate your client's position.

Avoid personal attacks in letters and other writing. While it may be appropriate to point out in a calm and objective fashion an opposing lawyer's improper tactics, endless letters by lawyers whining about their adversaries rarely accomplish anything for clients except to run up bills and aggravate otherwise unpleasant situations. Consider the following two examples.

A lawyer in a transaction falsely accuses you of having lied to him about the existence of a material matter. You can:

1. Write him a letter telling him that *he* is the liar and that you will report him to the bar. He then "gets even" by having his client tell your client to fire you. Lacking trust in anyone, your client decides to drop the transaction.

2. Write him a letter explaining that while he feels you have failed to properly disclose the matter, he is incorrect in his view because a full disclosure was made on page 27 of the purchase agreement, which you previously sent him. His client, seeing the letter, decides to pay more attention to your ideas than his. The transaction is closed without further problems, and your client is satisfied with your work.

Avoid writing letters that misstate facts or advance frivolous arguments. These types of letters are not helpful. Remember that your credibility is important and anything that undermines it can create problems for both you and your client.

Send copies of your letters to all appropriate parties,[21] including your client (unless otherwise agreed) and your supervisor(s). Also remember to see that a copy is kept in the case file and a chronological file if you keep one. By sending copies to everyone who is entitled to be copied, you will keep everyone up to date.

Lastly a word about threatening letters. These can get you into a lot of trouble. *Do not write a letter that could hurt your client's case or undermine your personal credibility if it were later shown*

---

21. Remember that the rules of professional conduct bar communication with a represented party without permission of his or her lawyer. *See, e.g.,* ABA MODEL RULES OF PROF'L CONDUCT R. 4.2 (2009).

to a judge or jury and/or published in the newspaper. Make threats only if you plan to follow through with the threatened action and if the action is both lawful and appropriate. Idle threats are usually transparent. Above all, do not threaten to go to criminal authorities if money is not paid. In most states, this is the crime of blackmail. If your client wants a harsher attack, tell him or her that you are a lawyer, not an extortionist.

TIMELINESS

It is important to get your written work done on time. There is probably nothing more frustrating to an assigning lawyer than to have a new lawyer miss a deadline. If more time is needed, consider working late or on a weekend. If you need help with the work, ask the assigning lawyer for it early on. If that is simply not enough, go to the assigning lawyer as early as possible and negotiate an extension. Never leave a lawyer or a client "in the lurch." You will pay too high a price—and so will they.

THE TOP TEN PERILS OF E-MAIL

It is often said with great wisdom that the pen is mightier than the sword. If this is true, then the power of e-mail (the "cyber pen") can be a thousand fold more powerful. For lawyers, e-mail presents a host of advantages in communications, but it also poses very serious dangers. Here are my top ten perils.

1. **Waste of Time.** Not since the creation of the television has a technological advance so threatened our efficient use of time. All of us are continuously looking at computer screens and PDAs to check our e-mail. Think of how many times a day you stop your work to look at e-mail and you will realize that even the best multi-tasker is losing ground at an incredible rate. The only cure for this addictive behavior is to set aside specific time for e-mail. Even if you set a timer for thirty minutes and check every thirty minutes, you will improve your efficiency without sacrificing efficient response time.

Before you send out an e-mail, think about whether it is important enough to justify wasting the recipient's time. Most lawyers receive up to a hundred e-mails or more per day. Is the subject of your e-mail sufficiently important to warrant further intrusion? With the exponential growth in the number of e-mails, we run the real risk that everyone will pay insufficient attention to any e-mail, even those that clearly advertise their critical nature.

Write short e-mails and convey your message clearly. Trying to read a long e-mail on a PDA is a lengthy torture and generally unnecessary.

Avoid global e-mails to large groups in your organization unless it is absolutely necessary. Remember, you are asking everyone in your organization to stop and read your e-mail. When you realize that is one-tenth of a billable hour multiplied by the number of recipients, you may think twice about sending an e-mail on a relatively trivial point or one that could be researched quickly. Send e-mails only to those who need to know and no others.

2. **Miscommunication.** The written word has always been a difficult medium to master. For that reason, lawyers and other professional writers have to spend a great deal of time revising their work. E-mail, however, invites the quick and unguarded remark shot through cyberspace and landing where you may least expect it. Here are some common examples:

- Lawyer A wants to send a compliment to Lawyer B. She quickly types an e-mail and does not read it thoroughly before sending it. Lawyer B interprets the e-mail as sarcastic and stops speaking to Lawyer A. Perhaps the e-mail was not carefully drafted and could be interpreted in two ways. As is usually the case in life, Lawyer B chose the worst interpretation.

- A lawyer sends a client advice *not* to do X. The word "not" is inadvertently left out, and the client proceeds to do the very thing against which the lawyer wanted to warn the client. Outcome: The client sues the lawyer for malpractice.
- In a jurisdiction with e-filing, a lawyer uploads an incorrect version of a memorandum to the court's server. There is no way to correct the error since the bad draft is now a public record.

The only cure for these problems is to prepare your e-mails as though they were well-crafted letters. If they are worth sending, they are worth reading and revising carefully. Don't be afraid to print them out and review them to ensure that there are no errors. Always think about the impression your e-mail will have on the recipient. When in doubt, call the person. In a telephone call, your tone, your further explanation, and your ability to receive input from the recipient will ensure the best communication, particularly in fast-moving situations.

E-mail "chains" also contribute to miscommunication. Readers frequently read only the last entry in the chain. This often leads to a misunderstanding of the context of the remark. If you keep this in mind as you engage in chain conversation, you may be able to avoid confusion, particularly on the part of those who are more tangentially involved. For example, in a long e-mail exchange, lawyers and businesspeople are debating the merits of doing a proposed deal. After a while, one person sends a transmission saying that it is time to make a decision. One of the lawyers calls the president of the client and asks if she is available at 4:00 p.m. for a meeting to discuss the matter further. She says she will check and respond by e-mail. She picks up the e-mail chain and replies to all with the one word "no." Everyone thinks that the deal is off, except the client's principal decision maker.

3. **Misdirection.** The ease with which you can send an e-mail to the wrong recipients creates frightening scenarios. For example, in response to a firm-wide inquiry, a lawyer solicits his colleagues' views on a certain judge. Some of the lawyers reply with negative and biting remarks. By hitting the "reply all" button, the remarks are broadcast throughout the firm and somehow find their way into the hands of the judge. The client, learning of the problem, fires the firm to avoid a bad outcome in the litigation.

Similarly, in a recent case, a lawyer sent a proposed order to a judge by e-mail. Another attorney, who had received a copy, hit "reply all" and sent an unhelpful comment to the judge.

The ability of e-mail systems to store addressees in groups is particularly dangerous. You may see only the label of the group and forget who is included in the group. It is essential to see exactly who will be receiving the e-mail before you launch it.

Watch out for forwarding e-mails, especially e-mail chains. Be sure that you know the entire contents of what you are forwarding. It may be that an earlier comment in the e-mail chain was not intended for viewing by the recipient of the later comment you are forwarding.

As a general rule, avoid saying anything personally negative in an e-mail. Assume that it will find its way into the wrong hands. Even though the courts have upheld the privacy of e-mail, there is a reputational risk involved every time you write something personally unflattering. There is no benefit in life to negative gossip. With e-mail, the risk is magnified.

Global e-mails are potentially deadly. They advertise you. In a big organization, people can form unflattering opinions about you based on anything from spelling errors to the quality of the issues you present in the e-mail.

4. **Leaving Indelible Marks.** Everything you write in e-mail is memorialized for eternity. It may be—or become—discoverable. When you wrote it, it may have been privileged. However, there may be a subsequent waiver of the attorney/client privilege. Or someone may nefariously send the e-mail to unwanted recipients. Additionally, please remember that once it is in your computer, it is virtually impossible to erase.

Be prepared to live with whatever you write. The larger the potential audience, the more you will have to live with it.

5. **Lack of Privacy.** If you use your employer's computer, you have no expectation of privacy in what you write. Unless you have the capacity to encrypt or at least password protect what you write, Peeping Toms with access to the system can see what you have written and to whom. Ouch!

Always password-protect important documents. Do not use the firm's computer network to discuss personal matters unless you have no secrets with respect to these matters.

6. **Lack of Security.** When I was a federal prosecutor, I learned that if you want to protect a secret, you must never tell it to anyone who does not absolutely need to know it. If you send an e-mail to anyone who does not need to know what it says, you are multiplying the risk of an inadvertent or deliberate leak. Even in the case of what you think is a direct e-mail to one recipient using an encrypted protocol (e.g., https://), a third-party hacker can intercept the data. In a profession that

requires its members to zealously guard client confidences, e-mail is a potential disaster.

7. **Dubious Disclaimers.** These days, everyone counts on form disclaimers about the confidentiality of e-mail communications, which are generally attached to the end of their e-mails. They think that these disclaimers will protect them against an inadvertent waiver of privilege. These disclaimers, which tell the inadvertent recipient to destroy the e-mail, are so ubiquitous that nobody really knows what they say or whether they protect against anything. No one reads them. And indeed, since they are all placed at the end of the e-mail, one has to doubt that they seriously deter anyone from peeking. If you have a significant issue that requires the protection of the attorney-client privilege, use a letter or a telephone call. The full extent of the cyber law on this subject is not yet written, and your client does not want to be a party to the case that ultimately writes it.

8. **Undelivered.** Suppose you write an important e-mail to a client, but the client does not see it because: (a) the client gets one thousand e-mails per day, (b) the client lives in a culture where e-mail is not reviewed with regularity or punctuality, or (c) the Internet system is not perfect, so it gets lost. A deadline passes while you are assuming the client has received the e-mail. This can result in confusion and possible lawsuits, at the very least. It is wise to be sure you have received confirmation from the recipient of important e-mails.

9. **Unfiled and Lost.** Unlike traditional paper letters, which have a long tradition of being filed in hard copy, electronic mail is not usually filed in a physical filing cabinet. It may be retrieved at high cost, but it could still be lost or difficult to find when you need it. Use electronic folders to keep

your e-mail organized (both sent and received). When the client complains that you never told him something essential to his case, you will need to find the e-mail fast. All e-mail providers I know give you the ability to file e-mails. If yours doesn't, change providers or use Outlook. Always label and file your electronic correspondence. And be sure to back up your data in the unlikely event that your firm has no automatic system to do so.

10. **The Metadata Trap.** Metadata is the radioactive waste of the digital era. It turns out that Microsoft Word and other programs store all revisions. So it is easy to see what revisions have been made to a document, when they were made, and who made them. Always strip metadata from files or send them in PDF format to avoid broadcasting your private thoughts and revisions.

Successful professionals will control the risks outlined above. Remember to always think long and hard before you hit the "send" button. The career you save may be your own.

PERSONAL ORGANIZATION

A good lawyer is organized. In this chapter, I will offer you a few simple techniques for organizing yourself. If you are a reasonably organized person, they will help you immensely and immediately. Of course, if your organizational skills are seriously deficient, you must also study the habits of other lawyers who are better organized and may even benefit from professional help.[22]

Organization is a broad term. You want to be organized in your thinking, your time, and your space. We have already talked about organizing your thinking when you write, and law school has devoted a great deal of time teaching you about organized thinking as well. So in this chapter, we will talk about organizing your time and space.

---

22. Depending upon the degree of your organizational impairment, a range of professionals, including organizational coaches, psychologists, and psychiatrists may be helpful.

MANAGE YOUR TIME INTENSIVELY AND EFFECTIVELY

The principal commodity of all lawyers is time. And whether it is charged on an hourly basis or not, it is critical to utilize it effectively. If, for example, your firm has a contingent fee case, your ability to complete the case successfully in a shorter amount of time is critical to the profitability of the case. If your firm bills on an hourly basis, your ability to complete assignments efficiently avoids write offs, which likewise affects profitability.

1. The fundamental principle of time management is to keep track of all of your time. This can best be done by putting a clock on your desk and marking down what you do every minute of the day. This method will inevitably reduce wasted time without any effort on your part because it will subconsciously force you to work. Keep a timesheet in front of you and mark down everything you do. If you are inefficient, the sheet will provide an invaluable source of data on where the problem may lie. If you do not keep a running timesheet, you will reduce your billable time and increase your non-billable time. Your work will also be inefficient.

You should remember that timesheets are essential—not only to your management of time, but also to the proper functioning of any firm that bills on an hourly basis. If you do not keep your timesheets current, you cannot honestly bill your time to clients. *So keep a running timesheet and finalize your timesheets every day.* Failure to submit timely timesheets prevents proper billing and costs the firm money. You may end up cheating a client, but more likely, you will end up cheating your firm and yourself. In any reasonably well-run firm, the cost of this bad habit becomes evident almost immediately in computerized reports. The result will affect your salary and your future with the firm. Obviously, if you want to become an owner of the firm, you have to think like an owner. Time equals money.

The reasons why people do not keep good timesheets are many. For some, it is no fun to do. Others are caught in the "procrastination syndrome" where delay leads to panic, which finally leads to motivation. Some do not understand the importance of timesheets. The list is endless, but none of the reasons is sufficient to justify the failure to develop the discipline. I assure you that after a few weeks of following the discipline, you will master the timesheet and improve your efficiency.

2. Limit distractions. If you work on ten cases in no special order, punctuated by incoming telephone calls, at the end of the day you will have accomplished less and recorded less billable time. Try to do research in blocks of time and return telephone calls all at once. Obviously, when you start, you will not have complete control over your time. However, by coming in earlier in the morning or leaving later at night, you may find that you can bill blocks of time more efficiently.

Closely related to the issue of avoiding distractions is completing work. Most of us are pulled in so many directions that we have a large number of projects in progress. My view is that wherever possible, it is better to try to complete one task before going on to other tasks. Often taking just a few minutes more will enable you to cross off a task forever. In this way, you will be able to reduce the clutter in your life.

3. Organize and prioritize your work effort. This organizational goal can only be achieved by spending a few minutes every day preparing a "to-do" list and marking the priority of the items. The list will enable you to focus on the most important things first without forgetting the less important things.

Remember, a "noncritical" assignment is still critical to the client, or the client would not have been willing to spend money on it. As you complete the assignments on your to-do list, cross them off or delete them from your PDA. Give yourself a pat on the back and keep going.

Today, technology can enhance your task lists. PDAs and computer software enable you to make lists that are easy to read and enable you to easily prioritize. If you like the fun of computers, computerized task lists are great and can be easily reorganized. If you like yellow pads, that is fine too. Post-its work; however, they may drive you nuts as you sit in front of a sea of yellow scraps fluttering in the breeze of the ventilation system.

4. Avoid excessive socializing. Gossip is the single most significant time waster on the planet. We all do it, but as an avid talker myself, I can assure you that it reduces productivity immensely.

5. Please avoid surfing the Internet. Explore cyberspace at night on your own time, not during the day.

6. Finally, always have plenty of work to do. If you are underutilized, you will be less efficient. If you are light on work, ask for more, or use the time for marketing and improving your skills.

MANAGING YOUR SPACE

Closely related to time management is management of your desk and office space. If you cannot find things quickly, you will waste time, increase your anxiety, and work on matters in the wrong priority.

Although a desk is one of the most important pieces of equipment a lawyer has, most lawyers spend little time organizing it. The result is that work gets lost and precious time is spent looking for things. Here are nine quick tips to help you organize your desk.

1. Try to keep the top of the desk clear of everything except the file on which you are working. Keep your projects in working files in the desk and mark them down on your to-do list. Take the file out when you are working on it and return it when you are finished. When the project is finished, ship the file to a file cabinet and keep (or have your assistant keep) a list of what is in your filing cabinets. If you follow the simple principle that your desk should be uncluttered, you will be more organized and will also show others that you are organized.

2. Stock your desk with all the supplies you will need. You do not want to spend time running out to get a pencil or a pen.

3. Make sure your telephone is convenient to use. You should have a notebook or computerized file with all billing numbers and office codes so that you do not have to bother your assistant unnecessarily to look up the information. Have your calendar and contact lists close at hand, either on the desk or your computer. Take the time to stay proficient in all the functions of your phone, including conference calling, call transfer, and speed dialing.

4. Use plenty of light when you work. Many of us rely on insufficiently lit desks that slow us down almost without our knowing it.

5. Place a clock on your desk so you can keep track of time, particularly when other lawyers visit you to gossip.

6. Maintain a single location on your desk for notes. A Day-Timer or notebook is ideal. A computer notepad is also excellent. Post-its and shreds of paper are terrible and will result in a loss of information and confusion.

7. Organize your computer so that the most important programs—such as word processing, calendaring, a contact information list, and computer research features—are easily accessible through "shortcuts." If your firm does not have basic programs, you should politely ask for them. Or, if necessary, buy your own.

8. Keep a picture of someone you love on your desk. It will always remind you of why you are doing all this work and will comfort you in the rare circumstance when something goes wrong.

9. Have an in-box and out-box on your desk. If papers come in, they should be put into your working files or into the out-box. Otherwise the paper will bury you and remain unattended. At the end of each day, if not sooner, make certain that the boxes are clear.

The organization of the desk, of course, extends to the office. With my apologies to some exceptional lawyers with whom I have worked, I find that for most people, a confused office reflects a disorganized approach to work. You need not be a neatness freak to recognize that a reasonably tidy office enhances productivity and shows your colleagues and clients that you are in charge of matters. In a world where impressions count for a lot, consider your desk and office an extension of your clothing.

PERSONAL DIGITAL ASSISTANTS

You should obtain a pocket organizer of some sort. Some firms offer their lawyers Blackberrys, iPhones or Palm Treos for this purpose. Otherwise find a digital assistant that is simple, inexpensive, and versatile. It should easily synchronize with your computer, preferably with the personal organization program on the computer. You can obtain a wide variety of bells and whistles for it, including wireless capability and financial calculation software. But you don't need all the frills to get enormous benefit from your PDA. In fact, if it is too complicated (like mine), it may drive you crazy.

Remember that most PDAs allow you to color-code your appointments. There are many ways that this feature can help you. It can help you distinguish due dates for pleadings from court hearings. It can help you keep better track of tentative dates rather than fixed ones. The list is endless.

SCANNERS

I recommend that you invest in one or more scanning devices to enable you to scan and organize cases, news articles, and other documents you may want to have at your fingertips.[23] Scanners are now so cheap that you can buy a fast one with an automatic document feeder for three or four hundred dollars or a cheap one for fifty dollars. It is a good investment that will enable you to save and organize a great deal of important information.

Scanning software, such as Adobe, combined with modern operating systems, will enable you to easily organize your scanned documents in files on your computer. By using keywords in the file names or tags, you will be able to effortlessly create a searchable database to retrieve your files.

---

23. Much is made of "going paperless." At this point, it is probably unnecessary and risky to go completely paperless. Although you can and should maintain papers in electronic folders, I would not throw away the paper just yet. I have done so myself, but it requires a good deal of time scanning and backing up data on encrypted hard drives. Though useful in retrieving data, electronic data management takes more time, if you hope to avoid risk of loss and maintain confidentiality.

PRECEDENT FILES

You should maintain research files and copies of all significant memoranda and corporate documents you prepare. This will save you an immense amount of work in the future because it will give you a starting point for many future assignments. I suggest using colored folders to keep these items clearly separated from client files. Alternatively, you can maintain these files electronically and save on paper.

TELEPHONE ETIQUETTE

I have always had a fear of the telephone. It is very hard for me to catch the emotional nuances of a conversation without a face-to-face interaction. To make matters worse, I never know whether I am going to be bothering the recipient of the telephone call. As a result, I often postpone making difficult telephone calls. However, over the years I have gotten better and better at dealing with the telephone, so I have some advice for new lawyers.

To begin with, please keep in mind that law firms are communication centers. The telephone is still one of the most powerful methods of communication. A large percentage of disciplinary complaints and malpractice lawsuits are generated, in whole or in part, simply by the failure of lawyers to return calls.

So the first rule is to return calls promptly. *All client calls should be returned within minutes or hours.* Since clients hate to be kept waiting to speak to an attorney, the business of the firm will suffer if client calls are not returned immediately. *All calls must be returned within twenty-four hours.*

Afterward, be sure to make a note of what was discussed in the call. Ideally these notes should be entered into a computer file so that retrieval is easy. I prefer to dictate or type such notes, not only because my handwriting is bad, but also because it takes less time.

When the call has produced an important decision, it is generally wise to send a confirming letter. To mix metaphors, it is better to cover your rear end than to be caught with your pants down.

When talking on the phone, you should smile and keep a pleasant disposition. The caller will sense your enthusiasm. Clients especially like lawyers who are enthusiastic about their cases and their business. You should always let them know how important their situation is to you. Clients also appreciate a little empathy now and then. For example, at the end of a long call involving a situation in which something bad has happened—or is about to happen—to a client, I always take time to say, "I am sorry this has happened to you. We will do our best to help you."

If you are the one initiating the call, it is usually advisable to take a moment to prepare a brief outline of what you will cover in the call. This method will structure the call, shorten it, and ensure that you cover the necessary points.

If a caller calls you and wants to hire the firm, always get the prospective client's name, telephone number, and address. If you open a file, you will have the essential information for communicating with her or him. If, for some reason, you do not end up representing the prospective client, then you can send a letter saying that you are not representing her or him. Indeed, if you do not send such a letter, the person may come after the firm for not diligently handling her or his case.

It is also imperative that you limit the first telephone call to a very general discussion, without discussing confidential information. Just get the names of all of the parties involved and the general type of representation that will be involved. It is essential to run a conflict check before the firm takes on the matter, and you do not want to receive any confidential information that might disqualify the firm from representing an existing client.

Set limits on the amount of time you spend on the telephone. Long calls eat up time and energy. Shorter calls show efficiency to clients. Use your clock. If the call is taking longer than fifteen minutes, ask yourself whether there is a more efficient way to communicate. Never be afraid of suggesting diplomatically to the caller that you would like to summarize the issues in a fax or e-mail and then continue the discussion.

SEXUAL ETIQUETTE

What I am going to say here will necessarily be contro-versial, but I am going to give you my own take on things without varnishing the truth. Although I know of many instances in which romance in the office has led to fine, lasting relationships, for the most part, it is problematic.

In the United States, the workplace is a highly regulated location, where sex can involve legal risk. So my advice is to avoid it. What might begin as an innocent flirtation can easily turn into a Title VII sexual harassment case, particularly in the cold scrutiny of hindsight.

New lawyers are particularly vulnerable to sexual harass-ment because of the vast imbalance of power between them and many of their co-workers. So I suggest that you politely, but firmly, decline to participate in any sexual conversation or conduct.[24] If the problem continues, report the matter to senior

---

24.   As a general rule, the use of crude language in the office also reflects poorly on you. Many people dislike listening to vulgar language, so it is best to avoid it.

management right away. Dealing with inappropriate conduct at the outset avoids more difficult problems later.

Beyond the pure regulatory issues, however, the law office is a workplace of uneven power. Genuine relationships are generally difficult to build in that environment. Even good relationships can wear thin when they are mixed with the complexity of a law office. Indeed, it can become really unpleasant if your relationship with someone in the office means that your personal life and your professional life have no boundaries. Everyone needs a break from the politics and stress of the office.

If the regulatory and psychosocial barriers are not enough to deter you, let me give you a few other reasons to avoid romance in the law office. You should assume that every romantic liaison within a firm will become office gossip within forty-eight hours, particularly if it involves an associate and a partner. Immediately the working energy of the firm is reduced by gossip and speculation. Additionally, if a spouse is being betrayed in the course of the relationship, everyone in the firm feels complicit when he or she encounters that spouse at the office or firm functions. This situation causes turmoil and potential humiliation for everyone. Sometimes the firm is even drawn into litigation between the spouses. The firm has to consider whether a lawyer who betrays a spouse is not also capable of betraying clients and the firm. And finally, some people (particularly those who are happily married) tend to look upon such behavior as morally offensive or degrading.

I do not, of course, rule out the possibility that an interoffice romance can result in a wonderful, lifelong relationship. I know of many of them. Nor can I say that people cannot "sleep their way to the top." It happens. But if you want to have a saner life and a better chance of getting ahead, the odds favor abstention. It is a big universe, and there are thousands of possible romantic opportunities out there. Choose wisely!

Discussion of sex, sexual orientation, race, and religion in the office is also dangerous. Without knowing it, you can easily offend someone. Better to talk about the weather, sports, and even politics (though watch out for politics).

You should be aware of and follow all the rules regarding gender discrimination, including (a) a basic knowledge of employment discrimination laws, (b) all rules of professional conduct against discrimination, and (c) your firm's policies with regard to sexual harassment. If your firm has no formal policies on sexual harassment, you should insist on helping it develop some. There are plenty of good models available.

If you do find yourself in a situation where you pursue a relationship with a subordinate in the office, it should be disclosed to the firm management so that steps can be taken to protect the firm and clients from problems incidental to the relationship. Many firms have clear nepotism rules or may wish to take steps to be certain that there is no appearance of professional impropriety.

If a supervisor becomes involved with a subordinate, it is imperative to separate them in the workplace. Not only is this legally sound, but it is ethically mandatory. To the extent that associates compete with each other, they should be judged on their merits; the objectivity of the judges should not be in question. When a supervisor has a personal relationship with a subordinate, it calls that objectivity into question. If it comes out into the open, everyone will feel betrayed.

One final note. Sexual involvement with *clients* is an increasingly regulated area of legal practice. Some jurisdictions have rules of professional conduct governing such relationships of which you must be aware.[25] The initiation of such relationships is appropriately avoided or at least left until the attorney/client relationship has concluded.

---

25. *See, e.g.,* ABA MODEL RULES OF PROF'L CONDUCT R. 1.8(j) (2009).

DOING WORK
YOU HATE

Work is not always fun. Sometimes it is tedious, and new lawyers get their fair—sometimes unfair—share of it. As a veteran of "scut work," here are my ideas on how to handle the work you hate.

1. You can refuse to do the work—either expressly or passively. Mutiny, however, is usually severely punished. Therefore I do not recommend this option.

2. You can focus on the role your work plays in the larger effort. The case, as a whole, may be very interesting, and your participation at the periphery may give you a front row seat to view the action. For example, new associates are often sent on "due diligence" missions to review documents as part of a large corporate deal. As a new associate, I was often sent on such missions. I initially disliked the work, but I always found something that became the center of attention as the deal

progressed. I also got to watch how big deals were done, even if my role was limited.

3. You should recognize that the time you are spending might actually have enormous benefits to you. It may lead to better economic statistics on your performance. Perhaps mastery of an apparently boring tax research assignment will become a springboard for learning more interesting things about the area of law.

4. You can delegate scut work to others. This is generally a bad idea for a new lawyer because it leads people to believe that you are lazy and not a "team player." The insertion of a new level of staffing also generally causes higher bills for clients and inefficiency in accomplishing the work.

5. You can ask for better work. This method is a good one if you can offer some kind of alternative for getting the work done. It should be done with sensitivity and only after you have proven your own worth. You don't want to be seen as seeking special treatment.

6. You can try to redefine the paradigm. That is, you may be able to develop a way to accomplish the same result without the tedious labor. Offering a creative alternative is not a bad way to establish yourself as a good lawyer.

If all else fails, do the work you hate for a while, and then justifiably ask that somebody else be assigned to do some of it. This is usually the best alternative and leaves everyone with a feeling that you are both a good person and a team player.

DEALING WITH OVERLOAD

If you are a good associate, you will sooner or later wind up with too many assignments from too many people in your firm. Here are some good ways to handle the situation.

You should first consider whether you really are overworked. Unless you are working nights and weekends, you are not really overworked in the eyes of most legal organizations. For better or worse, most lawyers work long hours at some points in their careers.

When approached by a senior attorney to do work, you should generally avoid directly saying no. It is better to respond by saying that you would like to work with him or her and that you have "some time." However, you want to make sure that you have "enough time" to complete the assignment in a timely and thorough fashion. You should then describe the assignments on which you are now working and state when they will be completed. Ask if the attorney would be willing to talk with those who have already assigned you work to help reorganize and prioritize the deadlines.

If you say no to a partner, you create an especially precarious situation. The partner may feel rejected or angry. You do not want that. If you are not working nights and weekends, the partner may feel that you are not a hard worker, particularly if she or he *is* working nights and weekends. On more than one occasion, associates have complained to me about their heavy workload; however, when I looked at their billable hour numbers, there was no support for the complaint.

Saying no to work is also inconsistent with the objective of showing yourself as partnership material. The partner cannot easily tell clients that the firm is too busy to serve them. If you want to act like an owner—and you do, because it shows you have the maturity to become a partner—you have to show that you recognize that dealing with the firm's workload is always your personal responsibility.

I am not advocating draconian working hours as a way of life. But if you are efficient, you will find that you can handle more than you ever dreamed possible.

Efficiency is critical. Most people, in fact, only work at a fraction of their real capacity. If you doubt this, just think for a moment how much time you spend every day at work (a) checking useless e-mail, (b) checking news headlines, (c) checking the stock market, (d) looking for items to buy on the Internet, (e) socializing with other lawyers, (f) calling your friends, (g) worrying about a problem that turns out to be no problem at all, (h) becoming overly reactive to emotional situations in the office or in your personal life, and (i) looking for files and notes. It is incredible how much your mind can hijack you even when you think you are focused on your work.

If you can use the techniques in this book to just improve your efficiency by 5 percent, you will probably be the most productive lawyer in your firm. Indeed, if you apply the same rule to your life, I guarantee you will achieve success beyond your wildest dreams. It is not just a matter of hours; it is a matter of organization and energy.

DEALING WITH STAFF

As I mentioned at the outset, it is important to deal with staff in a constructive manner. Here are some concrete ideas for working with the staff, upon whom you must rely, in a firm.

1. Remember that since you are a lawyer, members of the staff both look up to you and envy you. They are quick to see all of your imperfections, but they may be equally willing to follow your lead. You have to build up trust to overcome the envy. This may be a lifelong effort, and sometimes the dysfunction of the staff (or yourself) may make it impossible. Nevertheless, you must always make the effort.

2. Keep in mind that the staff members often know more than you do about the mechanics of the practice. You need their guidance and should never be afraid to show your lack of knowledge. Over-assertion of authority is seen as arrogance. Under-assertion of authority may be seen as weakness.

3. Always be polite. Never raise your voice. Remember, you are paid more for the aggravation than the non-legal employees, and the non-legal employees cannot yell back at you without risking their livelihood.

4. Always make an effort to praise the employees at least five times before criticizing them once. Find good things to say. This effort will motivate people much more and improve the working atmosphere.

5. Never criticize an employee (or anyone else) in front of others. It is degrading to the employee and demeans your stature.

6. Never set unrealistic deadlines. Telling a word processor that the deadline is 5:00 p.m. when the document is not due for three weeks is unfair to everyone. I like to ask employees to tell me what a fair deadline is; then I can safely demand compliance.

7. Try to avoid last-minute rushes. This is not only good legal practice, but it is essential to provide a healthy work environment for everyone.

Some lawyers compulsively revise documents until the last possible moment, flirting with malpractice, in a futile search for a perfection they will never achieve. Other lawyers procrastinate and can only work under an extreme deadline. For the staff, these lawyers are an impossible drain.

Even if you have managed to get by all of your life obsessively working down to the wire or using the pressure born of procrastination, it will not work well in legal practice, because the practice already has time pressure built into it. If you find that, notwithstanding your maximum efforts, you are chronically working until the last minute, you can improve your life and the lives of those around you if you get professional help from coaches, counselors, psychologists, or psychiatrists.

8. In dealing with secretaries, mail clerks, and runners, you should be authoritative, but never condescending. You can be demanding, but never demand anything that you are not willing to do yourself. Lead by example. Don't give a grueling, time-pressured assignment to a subordinate and take two hours for lunch yourself. Remember, the Thirteenth Amendment did away with involuntary servitude for everyone, except you! Your staff will try harder if you recognize that they are human beings.

9. Always show your appreciation for staff members and take a moment, if you can, to write them an e-mail or a note when they have done something really well.

10. If you find that you cannot deal with a staff member because he or she is rude or unpleasant, raise the issue with a supervisor. Do not try to deal with it yourself. Supervisors, if they survive, are skilled at dealing with these problems. You are probably not. Thus you are well advised to avoid unnecessary confrontations.

11. Finally, try to build loyalty among the staff with whom you work. Learn about their families, remember their birthdays, and try to encourage their development as people. If you see people with special talents that could be realized by education or different experience, encourage them. The best quality of an institution is that it promotes its people and challenges them to achieve the finest things of which they are capable.

Secretaries—or "legal assistants," as they are often called—are vital to the legal profession and deserve a special word. They are much more than typists. They supervise communication between lawyers and their clients, between lawyers and courts, and between lawyers and other lawyers. There is a vast network of secretaries throughout the legal profession, a network that often works together in a more collegial fashion than the lawyers. This network is responsible for much of the efficiency of communications in a business where communication is critical. You should recognize that good relationships with secretaries are very valuable to an associate. A partner's secretary may actually have some input into your own evaluation. Therefore, please treat secretaries like they are gods. You won't lose anything, but you may have a career to gain.[26]

26. In today's environment, it is normal to share secretaries with other lawyers. The need for diplomacy and skill in dealing with secretaries is now exponentially increased.

CRITICAL DEADLINES

Watch out for legally imposed deadlines. The most significant contribution that a new lawyer can make to the practice is to help the senior lawyers recognize and meet such deadlines. To do this, you will need to pay extreme attention to the calendaring of deadlines and to the completion of work well in advance of the deadlines. Senior lawyers are responsible for multiple cases and may not always be capable of watching out for hearings and filing deadlines the way you are. You will typically have only a few cases on which to work. Use the lack of clutter to help those whose lives, despite all organizational efforts, are impossibly cluttered. If you succeed, you will be indispensable. If you fail, you may be blamed, notwithstanding your innocence.

Here are a few of the deadlines I think are the most significant:

1. Any deadline imposed by a court order, including deadlines for disclosure and the filing of a pretrial stipulation.

(Preclusion of a key undisclosed witness can be an easy case of malpractice.)

2. Any deadline for filing a notice of appeal.

3. The deadline for responding to a complaint.

4. The deadline for removal.

5. The deadline for responding to an amended complaint.

6. The deadlines for responding to discovery. (Often failure to meet the deadline waives objections and may waive privileges.)

7. The deadlines for answering requests for admission. (Failure to meet the deadline may constitute an admission.)

8. The deadlines for post-trial motions.

9. The statutes of limitations. (Know the rules cold.) Many malpractice actions arise from missed statutes of limitation and appeal dates. See that these deadlines are met in every case. You will rarely be penalized for filing early.

10. The deadlines for giving contractual notices.

11. Statutory deadlines for filing tax returns, securities reports, and probate claims.

12. Any reasonable deadline imposed by a client.

Calendaring is a special art.[27] Today's computer software is quite helpful in the process, but I personally find that a double-entry system, using both a computer and a traditional appointment book, is the best. Once again, remember to consider using color-coding on your computer to distinguish different types of appointments.

---

27. Recognizing this, many large firms have departments dedicated to managing deadlines. These, of course, are no substitute for your own efforts.

Asking for extensions is common. But on balance, meeting deadlines rather than extending them leads to more efficient work and less cost to clients. Eventually the work has to be done anyway, and as I said earlier, procrastination is antithetical to performance. Of course, there are exceptions to the rule where there is a valid reason for delay—such as awaiting the results of a controlling case about to be decided in an appellate court—but these exceptions are few and far between.

THE ART OF NEGOTIATION

Virtually everything you do as a lawyer involves negotiation. It is as central to your life as planning; and yet, despite occasional efforts to teach this skill in law school, most new lawyers are poorly trained negotiators. Therefore I strongly recommend reading *Getting to Yes* (Houghton Mifflin, 1981) by Roger Fisher and his colleagues at the Harvard Law School, a book that analyzes methods of negotiation and teaches the subject clearly and thoroughly. Additionally, a later book, *Beyond Winning* (Harvard Press, 2000), by Robert H. Mnookin and others elaborates on Fisher's principles quite well and applies them specifically to the legal context. The following are a few pointers, however, which can help you right away.

    1. Identify quite clearly what role you are going to play in the negotiation. Clients usually negotiate the basic terms of deals. Sometimes, however, the clients may give instructions to the lawyers on what deal they want the lawyers to negotiate.

Either way the lawyers come into the picture to negotiate and draft contracts and other papers to document the deal and to allocate some, but invariably not all, of the risks. Your job as a lawyer is to watch out that your client gets what he or she expects out of the deal without hidden risks. However, too often lawyers create unnecessary obstacles to finalizing transactions.

2. Try to be sure that you, as a new lawyer, get input from more experienced lawyers on evaluating risks. A client is often well advised to take some risks. For example, in negotiating a purchase agreement in which your client is selling assets, fighting to the death on behalf of the client over the wording of a representation that the buyer has a valid corporate charter is not too valuable, if the client is going to get cash at the closing. (In this connection, I once spoke with a renowned corporate attorney who told me that he did not care what kind of a contract his client signed, if it had liberal termination provisions. His view was that the only thing that mattered in negotiating a good contract was the ability of his client to get out of it.)

Hardnosed, objective, and accurate evaluation of litigation risks is also critical to achieving the client's objectives. In litigation, more than in almost any other area, it is the lawyer who dominates the process because of superior knowledge of the technical aspects of the case. However, it is the client who ultimately pays. Winning in the litigation game is often overshadowed by the transaction costs of getting to the final result. So a good lawyer has to look early on for ways to control the litigation costs. Negotiation at an early stage, in my experience, often leads to better economic results for both sides of a case.

Of course, cases may be successfully litigated to the finish line in situations where broader policy considerations of the client dictate it. For example, an insurance company's policy of never paying fraudulent claims often inspires litigation to the death, and for a good reason. However, all too frequently, cases are litigated because the clients are successfully allowed by lawyers to commit themselves to the "game" of litigation and to reject negotiated alternatives.

3. It is always important to acquire sufficient information to evaluate your client's position early on. Investigation, early discovery, and legal research are critical here. But even more importantly, understand your client's true objectives. Does the client simply want revenge? Is the client willing to pay for the "Stalingrad" approach to litigation, in which every deposition is taken, every motion is made, and every tactic pursued? Clients may tell you that they want to pay, but in the end they will be angry if they have paid and not obtained an offsetting value.

4. Try to analyze any situation from the perspective of the other party. Remember, there are few negotiations that can effectively proceed by ultimatum. Although most negotiations involve some compromise to reach a resolution of the issues, it is quite possible to have settlements in which both sides win. Either way, successful negotiation can only take place if you can thoroughly understand the underlying interests of all of the parties.

It is a myth that all negotiation is a "zero-sum game" in which a concession on the part of one party is an equal benefit to the other. Lawyers who negotiate most successfully look for ways to strike agreements that are good for all parties. Therefore you should begin by striving to find a solution to conflict in which both parties can achieve their ultimate goals.

5. Negotiations are rarely constructive unless you prepare intensively for them. Work with your client to come up with a negotiation strategy before you begin negotiating. Develop a list of objectives you hope to achieve and prioritize them.

You will then be able to work with your client to see where you may be able to give up some ground to achieve the most important objectives. Also spend the time to develop a list of your adversary's probable interests and see how much you can accommodate those interests without serious sacrifice.

6. Keep your client and your supervising attorney advised of the progress of the strategy and your conversations with opposing counsel. There is nothing worse than making apparent progress in a negotiation only to have that progress undermined by your client's sudden recalcitrance when he learns, at the last moment, of concessions you have made on his behalf. You will easily lose your credibility as a negotiator, and the likelihood of the most successful outcome will diminish.

7. Always treat your adversary civilly, even when your courtesy is not reciprocated. Always act honestly. Deception is not only unethical, but it also undermines your credibility and obstructs the negotiation. It is wiser to have no deal than to trick someone into a bad deal. Fair negotiations generally lead to fair results. Be tough, but fair.

In a negotiation, you should always begin by listening carefully to the concerns of the other party. Spend time trying to ask questions to develop a clear understanding of your adversary's interests and positions. Not only is this inquiry helpful in your own analysis, but it also gives the adversary an opportunity to see that you are fair and reasonable, even if you do not agree. It also gives you an opportunity to think about whether there are ways of achieving "win-win" outcomes in which each party comes out ahead.

8. Always try to get your adversary to make the first offer. You will find that this generally leads to better results in the end for your client, even if the first offer is outlandish.

9. You will find it helpful to look for common ground between the parties and try to work at expanding the amount of agreement. In your communications, always keep your adversary focused on areas of agreement as a prelude to discussion of the areas of disagreement. Urge your adversary to look at the totality of what you are proposing rather than becoming too focused on the specific areas of disagreement.

10. Never overreact to apparent conflicts between the parties or lose sight of what is important to your client. When negotiating a deal, both you and your client must look at the totality of what the adversary is proposing. Often there are useful olive branches interspersed among the arrows. If you react too quickly—an all-too-common trait of new lawyers—you will lose important opportunities. You should take time to look at the whole package and avoid becoming totally bogged down in the details.

11. Never become consumed by rhetoric. Particularly in situations in which clients are present, lawyers often make passionate speeches to prove their allegiance and to show that the client's money is being well spent. If you focus instead on the economics of the deal and the underlying interests of the parties, the rhetoric will ultimately give way.

12. As a new lawyer, you will often have difficulty deciding which issues are really worth fighting for in a negotiation. Don't be afraid to say that you need to consult with another lawyer or with your client before committing to a position. Indeed, if you are confused, you can sometimes even get a candid insight from your adversary, depending on who it is. For example, you can ask, "if you were in my position, what would you do?" Good negotiators will answer the question in a less biased way than you might imagine. They do not want a deal that

falls apart because it is so unfair to one side that performance is jeopardized.

13. Carefully understand the economics of settlements, including their tax consequences. Parties often have complicated economic objectives. Understanding your client's economic priorities will vastly assist you in conducting a negotiation.

14. Use time to advantage. Figure out who is under the greatest time pressure. Often your adversary will be under a greater time pressure to reach a settlement, and you can "hang tough" until your adversary is willing to make more concessions to settle.

15. If you want a negotiation to succeed, focus on keeping the process fair and the other side involved in negotiation. After a while, their investment of time in the negotiation process may produce a solution to many problems. At the last minute, money may appear that was not previously offered. Parties sometimes make concessions just to get the deal done. Patience is therefore a virtue.

16. Always reduce settlements to writing as quickly as possible. Quite apart from the obvious problems with enforcing oral agreements, it is important that the parties understand the deal to which they have agreed and don't try to back out.

Finally, figure out when negotiation simply won't work. In Florida, for example, court-ordered mediation results in settling about 85 percent of cases. The rest cannot be settled. Don't waste time if your client insists, after objective advice, that there is no possibility of settling the case. Simply move on and wait for another point when the parties may have different views.

DEALING WITH SOBS

Like it or not, any profession that deals with individuals sometimes involves dealing with SOBs. In the course of time, you will find among your clients, colleagues, bosses, judges, and adversaries individuals who seem to want nothing more than to make your life unpleasant and humiliating. Some are constitutionally sadistic. Some want to advance their clients' positions by being unreasonable. Some are having a bad day. You may even find that you too are unpleasant to yourself and others. Here are some "routine" situations:

- A partner yells at you because the work you have done is not up to her expectations. Your memorandum is unceremoniously ripped to shreds or marked up into oblivion, causing you to have insomnia for a week.
- An adversary falsely tells your senior partner that you have lied to him about a material fact, and the partner seriously asks you if you lied.

- A judge accuses you of having deceived him when you plainly disclosed everything accurately on page 1 of your memorandum of law that the judge evidently did not bother to read.

- An adversary makes an accusation about your client in the press that is patently false, but the court rules and state bar rules prevent you from commenting in response.

- Your colleague claims credit for a piece of work you did.

- Your client calls and complains that you are wasting his time and money when you are on the verge of obtaining summary judgment in his favor.

- You did a fine job, but the judge was biased and ruled against you. You are beating yourself up because you think there was something you could or should have done to avert the result. You yell at your secretary.

- Your adversary claims falsely that you are withholding documents in a litigation when you have been making every effort to comply scrupulously with the discovery rules.

- Another lawyer accuses you of misconduct based on hearsay or a partial understanding of the facts.

How do you deal with these obnoxious people effectively? Here are few valuable tips I have learned from every bitter experience you can imagine.

1. Do not take what they say personally. However difficult the situation, you cannot extricate yourself successfully unless you can keep your cool. If you rise to the bait, the SOB wins. So don't do it. Respond to every negative statement in a composed and professional way.

Focus on the fact that the only thing that matters is your client's ultimate success.

2. Understand that SOBs (including yourself) act that way because they are uncertain of themselves. Under pressure to perform, everyone can lose his or her temper. It is almost never advantageous for you to throw gasoline on the fire.

3. Act politely and it will generally diffuse the situation. When a client yells at you because a judge has ruled against him, offer your sympathy and explain the options that may exist for settling the case or obtaining a review of the decision. If the client will not listen, try to ask questions that give the client an opportunity to vent her or his anger and ask what he or she wants you to do. Most difficult situations present options. The critical question is not how you got into the situation, but what option will maximize your client's position going forward.[28]

4. Try to find the grain of truth in the criticism and correct the problem when someone criticizes you unfairly (which will happen more than once). While it is sometimes necessary to set limits or to correct misimpressions, it never helps to get into an unnecessary fight.

5. Try to empathize with the person. For example, suppose that your senior partner has reamed you out for not properly researching a problem. You feel defensive and humiliated. Worse, you actually did do the research correctly. Try to respond constructively by saying something like this: "I sense you are dissatisfied with my work. I tried to do it right, but I want to make

---

28. This situation, of course, highlights the importance of explaining to clients beforehand the risks of litigation—including capricious judges and juries.

sure you are satisfied. May I do it over? I need some guidance understanding the issue. I looked at the problem you were raising, but it seemed to have been resolved by the Supreme Court of the United States. I will get you a copy of the case, and perhaps we can talk about it later, when you have some time."

Often simply listening to the person who is screaming and articulating his concern will calm him down. For example, assume that your senior partner comes back from a hearing having been degraded by a judge who sharply criticized a memorandum you wrote, saying that it was the worst piece of garbage she had ever seen. The partner comes into your office enraged and ready to yell at you. After listening for a minute or two, without reacting violently, you can respond in this way: "I'm sorry, Jane, that the judge beat us up. Not only that, I'm sorry you are also left explaining a difficult situation to the client. I sense you feel I'm at fault, and that if I had done better work, the matter would have had a happier ending. I am sorry, but I want you to know that I'll start on a motion for rehearing right away. Maybe we can still turn the judge around." By giving the partner some room to ventilate and showing some empathy, the steam tends to escape harmlessly into the atmosphere.

6. Set limits, when appropriate, on abusive and humiliating statements. If you are skilled at humor, you may be able to diffuse some of the tension with a calming and amusing response. But at some point you may have to tell the person clearly that you cannot deal with his or her anger or abuse. If you can, it is best in these situations to still make an effort to reaffirm the person with whom you are setting limits as a human being by saying something like this: "I very much respect you and feel bad when you are upset with me. It makes it difficult

for me to focus on the problem. Perhaps we can talk when I've had a chance to think about a solution."

Judges, of course, require special treatment. When dealing with judges who become abusive (and some do, routinely), you must always remain calm and deferential. Listen closely to the judge's words so that you can respond appropriately. Sometimes an outburst by a judge can lead to a fair recusal motion. Sometimes you can improve the judge's disposition to your client by complying with annoying but harmless directives. Never respond in anger. You are paid to listen, and your anger, if articulated, may result in disciplinary action against you or a penalty against your client. Stay calm. This too shall pass.

7. Be kind to yourself. When dealing with SOBs, particularly those for whom you work, the tendency is to focus obsessively on the conflict, rehearsing it over and over until you are sick. Of course, you have to respect your negative feelings; they are understandable. At the same time, my experience is that most conflicts will be irrelevant in two weeks. So *consciously* focus your mind on the bigger picture and match your angry emotions with equal time for positive thoughts about the things that are still going right in your life (including the fact that you are still alive). You will suffer less and help your clients more. I know it is easier said than done and requires practice, but mastering your reactive emotions beats the SOB every time and makes your life as a lawyer much happier. [29] Indeed, it is an essential skill of every successful lawyer.

---

29.   Remember that the process is like a "tug-of-war" between you and the SOB and between you and your own reactive emotions. If you drop the rope, the war is over, and the tension is released.

HANDLING MEETINGS

One of the most important things you will do as a lawyer is to participate in meetings. Even with the advent of e-mail, some meetings are inevitable for group processes to work.

The biggest mistake new lawyers make is to believe that at a meeting all you have to do is to arrive at the meeting, speak your piece, and convince everyone you are right. Actually, preparation for the meeting is far more critical to its successful outcome. Your skill in organizing and running meetings is one of the essential arts of law that is not taught in law school. Here are some tips that will help you.

The first step in the process is to determine whether a meeting is really necessary. Remember that meetings are quite expensive (consider the hourly rates of the attorneys, including preparation and travel time). Can the issues be decided by a telephone conference call? Often they can. But sometimes a face-to-face meeting is simply the most effective way of getting things done, particularly when there are too many parties involved or the parties do not know each other well.

Once you have decided that a meeting is necessary, determine who must be at the meeting in order to make the decisions required. After you have decided who *must* be at the meeting, decide who else *should* be invited. Here you have a delicate balancing act. Inviting more people to the meeting may serve many political agendas. Leaving people out is often bad form, but inviting everyone can make the meeting unwieldy.

Find a date that is convenient for everyone. This task is one best tackled by e-mail, requesting available dates. Often, if there are a lot of people involved, it is a good idea to consider delegating this effort to your legal assistant.

Next it is wise to develop an agenda for the meeting. Few meetings are effective if there is no agenda to follow. Without an agenda, the meeting may well be disorganized and fail to result in decisions that can be implemented. Ideally the agenda should be written and circulated in draft form in advance of the meeting to the participants so that everyone can have an opportunity for input.

If the participants in the meeting are going to make decisions based upon written reports, be sure that the reports are circulated well in advance of the date of the meeting. If you can get the participants up to speed before the meeting, you will be ahead of the game. In fact, the best meetings are those where the participants have prepared well enough that they can narrow the issues down to a bare minimum and where everyone has a clear understanding of the "decision tree."

You may also want to contact the participants individually ahead of the meeting to get feedback on the written materials and the issues to be presented. Lining up support before a meeting is often the most important thing you can do to ensure that it will produce the results you want. For example, before meetings at which votes will be taken, I like to contact everyone who I think will be a supporter of my cause to ensure that each of them will speak on behalf of the proposal. Sometimes a "pre-meeting meeting" can resolve a lot of the issues and allow the meeting to focus on the most important points.

Be sure that you follow the agenda at the meeting to the best of your ability. This will ensure that the important points are covered in an organized way. Keep good notes and prepare a memorandum summarizing the decisions that were made at the meeting.

At a meeting, it is important to let everyone say what is on his or her mind (within limits) and patiently listen to everyone's view. If you can find common ground, it will help a lot to smooth over the differences.

Seating at the meeting may also be critical. Normally you should give some thought to organizing the seating so that the senior decision makers have central seats.[30] However, you may find it a wise practice to have your adversary in a deposition seated with the best view out the window. Or instead you may want adversaries to sit on the same side of the table to deemphasize their hostility. And it goes without saying that you should have a room that is big enough to comfortably seat all the participants.

Try to adhere to time limits. Short meetings are generally more effective than long meetings and permit everyone to meet their schedules. In some situations, you may wish to suggest limiting each speaker to an allotted amount of time to speak,

---

30.   What constitutes a central seat depends on the layout of the room and the design of the table. Ideally it should be a position from which the leaders are easily visible to all of the participants.

but avoid being heavy-handed or you will undermine your support.

Offer appropriate food and drink so that there is no interruption of the meeting and people feel "cared for." Of course, you should be careful with the budget. Offering caviar to a client on the verge of bankruptcy while trying impress her or him with your frugal billing practices is a poor idea.

Always take a moment in the course of a meeting to get to know the people as personally as possible. Remember, trust is built up slowly. Even the most contentious meetings can end in lasting friendships. Eventually lawyers are often actually hired by, or receive referrals from, former adversaries. One way to improve the interpersonal atmosphere is to take breaks, where the parties can talk about something other than the matters at hand.

As noted earlier, carefully prioritize your goals and negotiating positions on the basis of your client's interests. If you do this, you can make compromises (with the authority of the client, of course) in a more rational way because you will know what is most important. It is a common mistake of new lawyers to think it is worth killing a deal over every position. In most instances, this is not correct. In fact, showing recalcitrance on every issue may only intensify the belligerent positions of the other side.[31]

If you are expected to speak at the meeting, you should consider preparing a slide presentation using a program such as Microsoft PowerPoint. For some strange reason, people tend to think you are a better speaker if you have a slide presentation.

---

31.   As I said in the previous chapter on negotiation, a new lawyer should read books on negotiation and observe others who have experience negotiating. It is an art.

Or maybe there is some truth to the view that a picture is worth a thousand words. Remember, you can also use an easel with a few graphics or notes to help underscore your points.

In making a presentation, I find it helpful to begin with a brief history of the current situation, unless it is well known to the attendees. This presentation can be followed by an analysis of the issues currently under discussion and the options that are available. You can end with a recommended course of action.

As a speaker, take care to make your presentation concise and clear. Be prepared to answer any questions that may come up. Speak deliberately. If you speak too fast, you will not be heard.

Always consider the impact of what you are saying on the listener. If the message is not positive, the listeners—particularly your clients—will be less likely to assimilate it. It is always better, when giving negative news, to set the news in its historical context and point out whatever positive features the situation provides without distorting the reality of the situation.

When presenting good news, be positive, but be sure to honestly point out any pitfalls that may still arise.

Try to avoid being arrogant in your presentation and give credit (even somewhat undue credit) to others (including your clients and their employees) for having facilitated a good outcome. You will make more of an impact by being somewhat understated.

The final aspect of meetings, which is important, is the "recapitulation" of the meeting. At the very least, there should be an oral summary presented of the issues discussed and the decisions reached. In addition, you should prepare minutes of the meeting, which can be circulated so that you can be certain everyone is on the same page with the decisions that have been made. These minutes should be circulated in some form shortly after the meeting. In some cases, it may be better to have this memorandum actually prepared and initialed at the meeting so there can be no dispute as to what was decided. The minutes should carefully set forth any assignments that have been given and the due dates for the completion of the assignments.

EFFECTIVE PUBLIC SPEAKING

As a lawyer, you will likely be called upon in your career to give oral presentations. When you were called upon to answer questions in your law school classes, you were given the opportunity to develop your public speaking ability to some extent. In your moot court program, you were given an opportunity to argue a case orally. But most law schools do not teach public speaking and do not directly measure your abilities in this often critical dimension of lawyering.

Most of us have learned public speaking either from watching others or being thrown into an experience where we had to swim or sink. Fortunately most people can swim. With a few tips, you will be fine.

1. Recognize that public speaking is stressful. Even experienced trial lawyers are nervous at the beginning of every trial or oral argument. The good news is that with very little experience and very little time, your nerves will calm down to

the point where they will be good motivators rather than impediments to your skills. So hang on just a bit. Speaking can be fun.

2. Accept the fact that you do not have to have a golden tongue to be a great orator. While it may be necessary to have a natural baritone voice and perfect delivery to be a television anchor, it is not necessary to be an effective speaker.

3. Rest assured that your audience wants you to succeed in presenting your point. If they have come to listen to you, they want to hear what you have to say. Everyone knows that public speaking is hard; you have the sympathy of your audience from the moment you begin. Only on the 24/7 cable networks do slight slips of the tongue become magnified into international crises!

My father was a brilliant orator and lectured to hundreds of students at a time. He was renowned for his ability to keep the students on the edge of their seats as he spoke dramatically about the most esoteric political theory. Furthermore, he could speak for fifty minutes (the standard college lecture) extemporaneously, or with perhaps three notes scribbled on the back of a napkin. Luckily almost none of us can do this. I say "luckily" because if my father's ability were required of all lawyers, most all of us would be out on the street.

Some of the greatest public speakers have not been perfect. President Obama is a fine speaker and gifted communicator, but he often uses a teleprompter or rehearsed lines. Abraham Lincoln had a high-pitched voice. Winston Churchill stuttered. The famed trial lawyer Gerry Spence is plain spoken but completely unpolished.

The key to effective public speaking is preparation. Even though my father did not write his lectures out, he knew ahead of time what he was going to say and in what order it would be presented. If you prepare, your presentation will be more than adequate. You can, of course, over-prepare and make your presentation too detailed. But when you start out, it is better to err on the side of over-preparation.

MASTERY OF THE MATERIAL

Before you attempt to prepare for an oral presentation, learn the material cold. There is no substitute for a complete understanding of the material. If you are in a meeting, you may get questions about your presentation. You want to be able to amplify without guessing or apologizing for your lack of information. If you don't know an answer, of course, you must say you don't know. But it is obviously better if you do. The more you know about your topic, the less nervous you will be and the more informative and effective you will be.

Remember: You do not need to be brilliant; you just have to know the material. If you do, you will appear to be brilliant.

PREPARATION OF THE PRESENTATION

To prepare, you have to decide what you are going to present. Sometimes you can choose the topic; sometimes it is chosen for you. In either case, careful organization of your points is essential.

Consider your audience. Lawyers have a bad habit of using language that ordinary people do not understand. Often they will throw out legal concepts that juries cannot comprehend (e.g., "the contract is a nullity because there was no consideration."). At other times, they use confusing jargon (e.g., "Even if the contract was not void ab initio, any damage suffered by the plaintiff was de minimis.").

Many lawyers may not realize it, but they almost certainly have a higher than average IQ; therefore, their command of vocabulary is greater than that of the population as a whole. Without speaking down to people, you can easily adjust your words to be certain they are comprehensible. To make this adjustment, record your speech ahead of time and review it, word by word. Then listen to newscasters. They tend to use vocabulary tailored to a wide audience. See what works for them.

It is important to consider what the audience needs from your presentation. Concentrate on the most important points from the perspective of the audience. For example, if you are giving a summation to a jury in a criminal case and you represent the defendant, concentrate on the high standard of proof (beyond a reasonable doubt) and the failure of the government to deliver that proof. The jury does not need lofty platitudes. They need help in concretely analyzing the proof and looking at its deficiencies.

Here is another example: Suppose that during an oral argument, the judge interrupts and asks you a question. Stop your speech and specifically answer the question honestly. Focus your remarks on the question itself. You can assume the judge understands everything else you have to say, even if he or she is not in agreement with it. You are there to deal with questions the judge may have; you are not there to give a great speech.

The best preparation for a public presentation, particularly a sensitive one, is to write out some or all of what you are going to say. If you do this, you will be able speak with confidence. This is particularly true if you are presenting sensitive material where slight changes in phrasing can make a lot of difference (e.g., oral arguments). Even if you ultimately speak extemporaneously, you will find that the discipline of having written out the argument will provide you with a solid foundation.

Organize your presentation. I usually like to begin with an introduction that succinctly sets forth the points I am going to cover in the presentation. Next I like to cover the background of the issues, such as the procedural history of the case. Then I take the points one-by-one and conclude with a summary.

DELIVERY

When delivering an oral presentation, new lawyers generally speak too quickly. Whether it is nervousness or inexperience, they talk a-mile-a-minute. Speak deliberately and calmly. You will get your points across in a more effective manner. If you cannot, based on time considerations, get to the same level of detail, it will make no difference. With oral presentation, you cannot expect the listeners to retain more than the basic points of the presentation.

Always get to the point quickly. Unless you are a good comedian, avoid wasting time on silly jokes and irrelevant material. If you finish early, take questions or sit down. It is what you say that can get you into trouble. What you fail to say will probably not get you into trouble. When in doubt, silence is golden.

Be humble. Your audience will always be more sympathetic with you if you are not pretentious, imperious, arrogant, and self-aggrandizing. You will also be less nervous because you will not set the expectations of impressing your audience too high. President Obama is a good example of a speaker who is successfully self-deprecating.

In the art of oral persuasion, carefully line up the rules to be applied with the facts of your case. More importantly, show that your situation merits favorable consideration. Show that a resolution favorable to your client is not only required by the rules (which can be ignored, distinguished, twisted, etc.), but is also the fair resolution of the situation given the private and public interests involved.

Avoid apologizing for your nervousness. Do not readily concede debatable points without having considered the concessions strategically.[32] Of course, answer any question truthfully and do not cling to unreasonable positions that undermine your credibility.

Avoid bad habits. Everyone commonly uses crutches such as "a," "um," and "and." It is difficult to avoid them, but professionals do. Watch TV and you will see. To get rid of these crutches, carefully record your presentation ahead of time. You will notice a host of nervous habits that you can avoid consciously, now that you have seen them from the perspective of the audience.

VISUAL AIDS

A great debate now rages about the value of video aids to oral presentations. Some think that nothing can be said meaningfully without a full PowerPoint presentation, replete with animation. Others shun glitzy electronics in favor of simple speech. There is no clear answer, except to focus on the purpose of the presentation. Short video clips of a deposition may be very helpful in front of a jury. Graphics of selected documents are very helpful in arguing motions.

---

32. The presumption should be in favor of the old debater's rule: "Admit nothing; deny everything; and shout loudly for proof."

What does not work is to overload your presentation with so much glitz that nobody can pay any attention to what you are saying. If you are in doubt, less is usually more. Remember that every time the audience is looking at a giant screen, it is losing the ability to hear you. And while science shows us that people can receive two messages simultaneously, comprehension diminishes in the process.

YOU ARE QUALIFIED!

The great trial lawyer Gerry Spence[33] has a training video in which he constantly urges new lawyers to remember that they are qualified and competent to try cases. I think this applies to all oral presentations. Yes, you are—and probably always will be—nervous about oral presentations. But you are qualified. Your presentations may not have the spectacular showmanship of my father. They will, however, succeed in their purpose and reflect well on you and your clients.

---

33. Spence claims to have never lost a criminal case in fifty years of practice.

ETHICAL ISSUES

Most law schools teach ethics; most bar examinations test your knowledge of ethics. So from the very beginning of your career, you will be held to a very high standard of ethical conduct. Unfortunately, I have found that most new lawyers are "at sea" with ethical issues. They do not take the time to reread the rules of professional conduct. They either miss issues completely or they make up their minds to challenge conduct that is permissible.

However sanctimonious it may sound, the answer is to read the rules and the interpretative opinions of the bar. There is no substitute for research. However, I am going to give you a brief overview of the most serious problems that I have found arise, starting on your first day at work. If you avoid these problems at the outset, you will avoid the vast majority of all malpractice and disciplinary problems.

HONESTY

I will not dwell on it, but it is obvious that a lawyer should be scrupulously honest. Judges, clients, and the public at large often believe that lawyers are dishonest. In all of your dealings, you must be more honest than anyone. Even then you may still be criticized for being dishonest. But you will avoid problems if you are up front with everyone and have plenty of proof that you were.

CONFIDENTIALITY

On your first day, probably in the first hour, you will acquire confidential information about a client. You must know that confidences of clients are inviolate, with very limited exceptions.[34]

To implement the rule of confidentiality, I recommend that you avoid talking about confidential information in any public place and with anyone in the firm itself who is not essential to the work. Secrets are kept best which are not shared. You should always avoid discussing cases in elevators, in restaurants, on airplanes, and even perhaps on cell phones.

At the outset of any representation, you should explain to your client the basic rules of the attorney-client privilege and the methods whereby it may be waived. If a client has brought a friend or spouse to an initial interview, it is essential that you

---

34.   *See, e.g.*, ABA MODEL RULES OF PROF'L CONDUCT R. 1.6 (2009). The exceptions generally deal with conversations with the client about future violence by the client, utilization of the lawyer's services for fraudulent ends, and certain other unusual situations where public policy overrides the privilege. You need to consult the rules of your state for specifics, since they vary from state to state.

explain the rules and ask the unrepresented party to remain outside so that the privilege is not waived.

If your client seeks to discuss privileged information in the presence of non-clients, politely terminate the conversation. You do not want any claims that you caused a waiver of the attorney-client privilege.

If your firm is doing securities work, you should pay particular attention to avoid any situation in which you can be accused of trading on or disclosing inside information. It is best to consult with the manager of your organization before making investments in any company that may be a client. Many firms have committees whose function is to inform lawyers when it is "safe" to trade. Please be careful.

CLIENT SELECTION

The single greatest threat to a lawyer is a bad client. Such a client may lie and embarrass the lawyer, but embarrassment is the least of the problems. In some cases, you may be accused of complicity with the client, with obstruction of justice, or with fraud.

If you choose your clients wisely, you will not have such difficulties. The challenge, however, is that your first clients may not be blue chips. They may be individuals whose integrity is not assured. Here you have to exercise judgment. Everyone is entitled to counsel, but if the client is enlisting you to participate in a fraudulent scheme, you do not want the work. The torment of living with a client engaged in an ongoing crime is not worth any amount of money.

To vet a client, ask questions. What does the client do for a living? How long has he worked at the job? What is the client's history? Is the client trying to change lawyers? A change of lawyers midstream is always a red flag. The client may well have had good reason to change, but if you do not fully understand that reason, you may regret it.

In the case of vetting prospective corporate clients, you may want to get a Dun & Bradstreet report, check one of the many rating and regulatory agencies, and run a Google search on the prospective client. If nothing else, you will show that you took appropriate steps to avoid a dishonest client should the issue ever arise.

Avoid high-risk representations. I hate to say it, but criminal defense involves legal exposures that are generally unacceptable, even for experienced lawyers. The clients may, of course, be criminals. They have incentives to turn on their lawyers to save their own skins. The fees they pay may come from illegal sources. Furthermore, prosecutors are often eager to charge criminal lawyers with obstruction of justice and other crimes arising out of the representation. After all, to some degree, stopping the wheels of justice from running over your client is your job as a criminal defense lawyer. That means any charges against you for obstruction must turn on whether or not your intent was criminal. Are you prepared to rely on your adversary to be objective about your intent?

Other high-risk representations include failing financial institutions, public offerings of stock in startup companies, and foreign companies with which you are not well acquainted.

Avoid undertaking representations for which you are unqualified, particularly in highly regulated areas, such as securities. Of course, you can work with qualified attorneys in such situations and learn from them. Without supervision, however, you are walking through a minefield.

Avoid clients who want to bring litigation for improper motives. Despite the common belief, you are not a hired gun. You are a lawyer whose responsibility is to avoid multiplying litigation costs without a good reason. Rule 11 of the Federal Rules of Civil Procedure and the steady stream of cases decided under it are good starting places for understanding your role. Investigate facts before you present them in court, and make a good record of that investigation in your file before initiating litigation. Remember, litigation may be fun and profitable for you, but it is a torment to those who are sued. Strike hard blows, but be certain they are clean ones.

CONFLICTS OF INTEREST

You might think that vetting new business prospects is not in your job description as a new lawyer. This is far from the truth, however. It is not uncommon for a friend or member of your family to hear that you have become a lawyer and to send a referral. Business is generated in the strangest ways. You may well be called upon to field new business calls.

As I said earlier, always perform a conflict check before taking on any work or discussing the details of a proposed representation with a prospective client. Your firm should be maintaining a centralized database for conflict checks, and you should enter the names of all parties before obtaining confidential information or undertaking a representation. If questions arise, it is wise to carefully review the conflict rules[35] to be sure of yourself before accepting or declining a representation.

---

35. *See, e.g.,* ABA MODEL RULES OF PROF'L CONDUCT R 1.7-1.10 (2009)

Always enter into your firm's database the names of any party with whom you have had confidential attorney-client communications before you have the communication. This is a common oversight that can lead to catastrophic consequences. For example, let's assume you have an initial meeting with a prospective client. The client provides you with a variety of confidential information. If you have performed no conflict check, you may miss the fact that the firm is already representing the adversary and may now be disqualified from that representation by virtue of your conversation. If you do not enter the name of the prospective client with whom you have spoken, you may find that your firm is not hired by the initial client but by his adversary. This may also lead to disqualification.

As a matter proceeds, it is not uncommon for new parties to come into the proceedings. Each time this happens, be sure to rerun the conflict check. When you think about new parties, think conflict.

On the other hand, not everything that seems like a conflict is a conflict. Be aware of the specific rules of your state. In general, you cannot take on cases adverse to existing clients without a written waiver. With regard to former clients, you cannot take on matters that are adverse and substantially related to the prior representation unless the former client consents in writing.

Always be conscious of the potential conflict of interest involved in any representation of more than one client in a matter. All clients should be advised in writing of both the benefits and risks of multiple representations (including possible waiver of the attorney-client privilege if the clients part ways).

Be aware that some representations may present business conflicts. For example, a securities defense firm may find it difficult to obtain work if the firm undertakes a major plaintiff's class-action suit against a brokerage house. Even a dog knows not to bite the hand that feeds him.

CONFLICTS ARISING FROM JOB CHANGES

There are specific and complex rules for conflicts arising from situations in which you or another lawyer in your firm has changed jobs. In some instances, the representation by the former firm of adverse parties can disqualify the new firm from an existing representation. In some instances, however, a "conflict screen" can be set up to wall off the new attorney and preserve the representation.

Most, though not all, conflicts can be waived by clients. Such waivers, however, must be knowing and clear. You must be careful to explain to clients the issues involved in the waiver, including the disciplinary rule, the facts that invoke it, and the consequences of a waiver. All of this should be in writing, signed by all clients. Waivers are always construed against the attorney, so make certain that you have dotted your "i's" on such waivers.

RETAINER AGREEMENTS

Always obtain an executed written retainer agreement at the time you undertake a representation. The agreement must specify clearly the scope of the representation. Otherwise the client may claim later that you neglected elements that did not appear to you to be your responsibility.

The agreement should spell out in detail whom your firm is representing and whom it is not representing. For example, if you are consulted by a group of investors in a business, it is important that they know and you know which party you are representing. Otherwise a disgruntled party may sue you, claiming that you agreed to represent everyone—or worse, that you were hired as the attorney for "the deal."

Retainer agreements should also spell out fee arrangements very accurately and completely, including the firm's billing policies with respect to costs. You do not want any misunderstandings. Some jurisdictions require the insertion of an arbitration clause in the agreement so you and your client can settle any disputes that may arise in an expeditious manner. If it is not required, however, I generally think that arbitration of client disputes is a bad idea. Arbitrators almost always want to split the difference after a trial. Courts, on the other hand, are likely to toss out frivolous cases before trial.

Retainer agreements should also spell out any potential conflicts of interest and the consequences that will ensue if they arise. This is particularly important in cases involving multiple representations, where you may want the parties to agree that in the event a conflict arises, your firm will be able to continue to represent one of the parties.

CLIENT FUNDS

Handling client funds is a critical task of lawyers, although new lawyers generally do not supervise this aspect of the work. Learn the trust-accounting rules of your jurisdiction carefully. Avoid comingling the firm's funds with the client's funds. Never "borrow" a dime from trust funds. To do so is a capital offense for lawyers. Always maintain the required records. Finally, use the trust account only for legitimate reasons pertaining to the representation. Please avoid the client who wishes to use you as a banker to pay bills or to make anonymous purchases. Money laundering is a serious offense, and you do not want any part of it.

ACCEPTING CURRENCY

I strongly recommend against taking currency. Technically there is nothing illegal about taking currency if it comes from legitimate sources and if you file a Form 8300 with the IRS (for amounts over $10,000). However, the client who wants to pay you in currency may have something to hide or may want to blackmail you with claims that he paid you money you did not report to the firm or the IRS. Tell your clients that you only accept checks or wire transfers.[36]

DEALING WITH SUPERIORS

Many times ethical problems arise and new lawyers attempt to bring them to the attention of their superiors only to be brushed off. This is a persistent problem in many law firms, and I have a few suggestions that may be helpful.

1.   You should never bring an ethical problem to a senior lawyer without having spent some time looking up the applicable rule and doing some research on the problem. Your presentation will be vastly better if you can back up your analysis with the current rules and authorities.

2.   You should never allow personal considerations to color your view of ethical issues. Sometimes new lawyers jump to the conclusion that a particular course of action is impermissible

---

36.   Also avoid "structured transactions" in which a client pays a single bill with multiple cashier's checks under $10,000. Such multiple payments suggest (the government might say prove) that the client is using currency to purchase the cashier's checks without triggering bank currency transaction reports.

because it will save them work if the action is not taken. When you find an ethical problem, always look for possible solutions. To take an obvious example, if there is a conflict in taking on the representation of an acceptable client in a cause you don't personally like, you should still consider whether the conflict could be waived.

3. If you disagree with your supervisor's view of the issue, you should tactfully ask if you can consult with the firm's ethics specialist. Most firms have one.

4. You must recognize that some jurisdictions exonerate a subordinate lawyer if the lawyer acts in accordance with a supervisory lawyer's reasonable resolution of an arguable question of professional duty.[37]

5. You may, if all else fails, refuse to perform the prohibited act. This is truly a last resort and will generally not be necessary if you have diplomatically followed the previous steps.

PAYING YOUR TAXES

One of the most serious problems lawyers face is the failure to pay their taxes. For several years, I was in charge of prosecuting tax offenses in South Florida. It was astounding to me how many lawyers simply failed to file any tax returns. I think this failure started with the pressures of the job, which made it difficult to find time to fill out the forms. The chore got put off. Then the lawyers became afraid to file because they thought, incorrectly, that they were going to get into trouble by filing late. It is an insidious disease endemic in the society.

---

37. *See, e.g.,* ABA MODEL RULES OF PROF'L CONDUCT R. 5.2(b) (2009).

I think the best solution to tax returns, even for a new law-yer, is to hire a CPA to prepare your returns. This idea may sound like heresy when your salary is low and you have ready access to computer programs like "Turbotax" to generate the forms. However, a CPA can:

1. Keep you on time by reminding you to gather all the information necessary for the preparation of the returns.

2. Ensure that correct returns are prepared and that pro-crastination is avoided.

3. Suggest legal ways for you to plan your financial life so that you maximize your income and lawfully minimize your tax burden.

4. Add her or his signature as an important verification that the return has been correctly prepared. It not only em-phasizes that you are a responsible taxpayer, but allows you to rely on that verification should anyone question the return (assuming that you have provided accurate information to the CPA).

Be sure to go over with your CPA all of the taxes to which you may be subject. Here, I especially have in mind household employees. These individuals are generally subject to FICA tax. You do not want to be grilled by anyone on why you did not appropriately pay or withhold this tax. There has simply been too much publicity about the issue, and the amount of money involved is generally minimal.

MENTAL ILLNESS AND DRUG ABUSE

You cannot honestly hold yourself out as a lawyer if you are suffering from a serious mental illness that impairs your ability to function or from abuse of a drug that is illegal. Statistics vary, but a very large percentage of disciplinary actions filed against lawyers involve alcohol and drug abuse. Lawyers also have exceptionally high rates of depression and substance abuse.[38]

It is beyond the scope of this book to deal comprehensively with the issue of how to control stress in your career. Some stress is inevitable. However, you must get help with alcohol abuse, drug abuse, and mental illness if they occur. Otherwise you will be lying to everyone about your ability to function as a lawyer. It is possible to have serious problems and still function to some degree. The issue, then, is when to take action. Here are some rules that may help:

1. Never use illegal substances. The consequences of violating this rule may ruin your life, as well as your career. If you are at a party and are offered drugs, leave the party.

2. Get help if you chronically drink more than two to three alcoholic drinks a day or if those around you are concerned about your drinking.

3. Never drink and drive. Newspapers and prosecuting authorities will cut you no slack for any violation because you are a lawyer.[39] And since the limits for blood alcohol are so low that a single beer might cause you to fail the test, just say no. (If you cannot avoid drinking when you drive, get help immediately.)

---

38. Depression is endemic in the general population as well; however, lawyers tend to be unhappier than other occupational groups. William W. Eaton, et al., *Occupations and Prevalence of Major Depressive Disorder*, 32 J. OCCUPATIONAL MED. 1079, 1081 (1990); Seligman, et al., *supra* note 1; Leonard L. Riskin, *The Contemplative Lawyer: On the Potential Contributions of Mindfulness Meditation to Law Students, Lawyers, and Their Clients*, 7 HARVARD NEGOTIATION L. REV.1, 10 (2002); Susan Daicoff, *Lawyer Know Thyself: A Review of Empirical Research on Attorney Attributes Bearing on Professionalism*, 46 AM. U. L. REV. 1337, 1375–85 (1997).

39. This, of course, is just one aspect of a larger issue. As a lawyer, your conduct outside of the office should always reflect well on you and the organization with which you are affiliated.

4. Avoid drinking alcohol at all public functions. It will likely impair your ability to use the functions to market yourself well. It will also slow you down and prevent your remembering critical information you acquire at the functions.

5. Get a professional psychological evaluation if you find that you have an eating problem, are missing appointments, or are too tired to go to work. These are typical symptoms of depression and will become a threat to your health and your clients' interests.

Compassionate help is available in many places today for those who seek it. All states have lawyer assistance programs and confidential hotlines. Alcoholics Anonymous is listed in the phone book. Finding a psychotherapist is not too difficult. It is better to get help early than to wait until something terrible happens.

If you are impaired, turn your work over to another lawyer. Do not risk hurting a client. You would be surprised how forgiving a law firm can be toward lawyers who have the courage to face their problems. There are plenty of recovering alcoholics and former drug abusers in top law firms. What cannot be tolerated, however, is the lawyer that resists treatment and insists on carrying on in the face of impairment.

TRADING IN SECURITIES

One of the greatest areas of risk for a lawyer and a firm is trading securities on inside information. I cannot stress enough that any securities purchase or sale you make should begin with an inquiry about whether the firm has a role with the issuer that precludes the trade. Most firms have rules to deal with this issue. If you have any doubt whatsoever, contact a lawyer with securities expertise to advise you.

THE ART OF SERVING
CLIENTS

On my first day on the job as an attorney in a legal aid office in a dilapidated part of New York City appropriately known as "Hell's Kitchen," I was following a veteran attorney to learn the ropes. We received a panicked call from a client of the agency telling us that he and his belongings had been literally thrown into the street by thugs. He was calling us from a pay phone. The legal aid office had been representing him in court in a landlord-tenant dispute in which his landlord was trying to evict him from a single-room-occupancy hotel in order to make room for a brothel or other "more lucrative" business. Apparently the landlord had grown weary of the litigation and thought that some "self-help" was in order.

We immediately went to the scene. The client was standing in the gutter in front of the seedy hotel with all of his worldly belonging strewn on the sidewalk. He was crying, and people kept walking by ignoring him, as we often do when confronted with poor persons in calamitous circumstances.

The attorney began by calming the client down, assuring him that we would get some help. He carefully interviewed him as to what had happened and immediately called the police. They arrived and he calmly explained that there was a civil case pending and that the landlord had decided that he did not want to follow court procedure, but instead wanted to use thugs to assault our client and to drive him into leaving his one-room apartment. The police promptly told us that this was a "civil matter" and that they could not intervene.

Undaunted by the unwillingness of the police to enforce the law or protect our client, the attorney went into the hotel and spoke to the "manager." He calmly explained that this was a serious violation of the law and that we would immediately go to court to obtain an order restoring the client to the premises. He reasoned with him at great length about the expense of litigation that his conduct would cause and its ultimate futility. Instead he suggested that they let the client back into his room for a few days until we could work everything out in court. The manager called the landlord, and the client was allowed back in.

I begin with this story because it shows the complexity of providing good service to clients and because it stands out in my memory as one of the most skilled legal services I have ever seen performed. Service to clients is the heart of what we do. It is an art requiring a lot of practice and skill. Yet in spite of the importance of experience, as a new lawyer, you can make a great difference to the quality of the service your clients receive.

Quality service to clients requires a fierce determination to achieve your client's legitimate goals. It often requires courage and creativity, especially when the chips are down, your cause is unpopular, and your skill is the only thing that stands between your client and injustice.

All clients deserve your respect because they have entrusted their important personal matters to you. It is also important that they feel your compassion and empathy with their situation.

At the same time, you have to balance your empathy for a client and your fierce loyalty with objectivity. No matter how trying the circumstances, you have to remain calm and think through what course of action will best advance the client's interests.

You can only be objective, of course, if you are scrupulously honest with the client, yourself, and everyone else. At every stage, you must be realistic about the situation and your own abilities. You may want to handle a matter for a client, but you may not be qualified. The client may want to sue someone, but you know the client will lose the case. The client may be entitled to legal redress, but the cost of obtaining it will be too high. The client might get off at trial, and you believe that the client was led into criminal acts by duress. Nevertheless, the client is ill advised to turn down a plea bargain involving some jail time. The list is endless, but honesty is the most important element in properly serving the client.

Skill is the next important component of service to clients. Be sure that you are always prepared to provide competent service. Some skills you learn on the job. Many are simply a matter of study. As a new lawyer, it is critical to study and prepare. The more you study and prepare the better service you can provide. Don't be afraid to ask questions of more senior lawyers or to watch them in action. There are no dumb questions. There are only dumb lawyers who are afraid to concede their lack of knowledge.

Showing clients that you are willing to work hard on their matters is essential to establishing a good relationship with them. Even if you think their problems are not urgent, they do not share this view. They are paying good money and want to feel that they are the focus of your attention. Do nothing to show otherwise. If you procrastinate with the work, you will not appear to serve their interests.

Responding to client telephone calls on the most urgent basis is essential to the functioning of a law firm, whether public or private. The failure to respond to telephone calls is a leading factor in malpractice actions. Clients generally understand the uncertainty of legal processes, but they do not understand unresponsive lawyers. If you receive a client telephone call, answer it within one hour or less. If you cannot do so, have your secretary or another lawyer call the client and explain that you are tied up for a few hours and ask the client if he or she can wait. Usually it is no problem. But unless the call is made, he or she will feel rejected.

Pay attention to the written work that goes out to clients. It should be a professional product, even if it is not a final product. "Rough" drafts make the firm look bad. Drafts sent to clients should have no typographical errors and should look like a finished product. Do not leave out essential elements in the project without speaking with the client first. A purchase agreement should look like a purchase agreement and not a set of boilerplate representations and warranties. A brief should look like a brief with a cover page and not simply Points I and II of a brief. Everything you turn out reflects on you and your firm.

Make sure that the work is done on a timely basis. When you promise a product, produce it well and produce it on time. Clients become frightened by last-minute productions. Moreover, they may want to have an opportunity to reflect upon and to comment on a draft of what is going to be submitted on their behalf. (By the way, senior lawyers are not too different in this respect.)

Sometimes it may be important to set limits with clients, but setting limits must be done judiciously. I once heard of a client who called on a Friday afternoon to ask a young associate if he could produce a memorandum on an important topic by Monday. The associate, keen to get to a basketball game, simply told the client that it could not be done. The firm, of course, lost an important client when the client went to a competing firm that put enough lawyers on the project to meet the deadline.

In this case, there was no doubt that the first firm could have met the deadline, but the young associate wrongly assumed the client was asking whether *he* could make the deadline—and he had plans to watch basketball. In fact, had he notified a senior lawyer, that lawyer could have arranged to meet the client's needs.

If a client imposes an unreasonable time demand, try to negotiate the deadline by finding out why the product must be produced on such a schedule. Often you can find other ways to serve the client's interests. Only as a last resort, tell a client that her scheduling objective cannot be achieved. You are paid to achieve it.

Believe it or not, billing clients is a significant part of the service you provide, even though you do not charge for it. Every month your bill provides, or should provide, a clear, concise statement of what your firm has done for the client in addition to explaining the cost of the services. Lawyers are generally very poor advocates for the extent and quality of their service, and failure to send timely and informative bills is a reflection of that poor advocacy. Remember, too, a client will never be more willing to pay your bill than the earliest possible moment that you send it, while the work is fresh in her or his mind.

Be concerned about billing clients excessively. Legal fees are always high, and clients do not like to pay them because they resent the fact that they need lawyers. After all, if people behaved themselves—the theory goes—there would be no need for lawyers. In this sense, there always exists a tension between you and your clients. The lawyer's interest may well be in spending time on a client's matters because it adds up to billable hours and, perhaps, a better result for the client. The client's interest may be to have an adequate, but not extravagant, effort. The use of contingent fees does not eliminate the tension, but it changes it. Here the lawyer has an interest in an early, if insufficient, settlement because it provides the greatest return on the time spent by the lawyer. The client may do better to litigate the matter to a conclusion.

The best way to handle the financial tension between client and lawyer that is inherent in the relationship is to put the matter on the table in a forthright manner. Collaborate with the client on controlling costs. By "partnering" with your clients, you will have fewer disputes over fees and a better chance of more work in the future. If there are going to be extraordinary costs, notify the client at an early stage so that he or she will be prepared to see them on the bill.

As a new lawyer, mastering the art of cost control is difficult and important. At the very moment you are struggling to produce perfect legal work in the face of your inexperience, you are asked to make sure that the work is efficiently produced. I suggest that you treat senior lawyers as your partners in the effort and jointly work with them and the clients so that your time will be profitably spent and your clients will be satisfied with the cost.

Build the client's confidence in you. Show that you work hard and know what you are doing. Never lose sight of the fact that clients need results, not simply your "product." You should, therefore, present all results (good and bad) in a timely fashion so that they can engage in strategic decision making, including whether to continue to retain you. The more they participate, the more they will understand the vicissitudes of the process and the need for you to spend time on it.

Much has been written on the subject of "total quality management" as a mantra for improving the relationship between producers and customers.[40] I commend it to you without necessarily endorsing much of the hype that has gone with it. The fundamental point is that the entire organization, from top to bottom, has to commit itself to innovative efforts to produce a better product for the customer. Again, the problem with this approach is that in the legal profession, the product is not really enough. It is a prerequisite to customer satisfaction without being sufficient to ensure it. The client may win without a brilliant brief. The client who loses will take small consolation in a brief that would have made Brandeis proud. It is therefore necessary to go beyond the product, to search innovatively for

---

40. A number of books on "TQM" are available free at http://books. google.com, including PERATEC LTD., TOTAL QUALITY MANAGEMENT: THE KEY TO BUSINESS IMPROVEMENT (Chapman & Hall, 1994).

ways to accomplish your clients' objectives, and to make clients feel that they are getting their money's worth.

You can achieve the clients' goals in a number of ways. You can improve the results by improving your general skill at the law. You will also increase your odds of success by carefully presenting your clients' positions to the world in ways that show them to have genuine merit. If you commit yourself to evaluating your own performance on the basis of the results achieved, you will continually improve. I believe firmly in adopting the adage that a good advocate can win every case. If something goes wrong, please examine honestly how it could have gone better, without berating yourself. If you find that you lose frequently because of external forces (bad judges, bad lawyers, etc.), it is wise to reflect further about where these losses are originating.

A special word should be said about foreign clients. They are usually unprepared for American litigation and corporate drafting. They often either micromanage it in a way that is disastrous or they are unwilling to comply with disclosure burdens, which run counter to the confidentiality that they normally enjoy in their own countries. In any event, representation of foreign clients will be a problem for you unless you constantly educate and prepare them for the process in the United States.

Let me end with one final note about working with inside counsel. Those who work in corporations are often very good lawyers. They may have expertise far beyond yours in areas of law of particular concern to their companies. Always treat them with respect. They are not stupid and will rightly resent any slight. Also keep in mind that their objectives are tempered by a set of corporate demands with which you may not be familiar. For example, the company may prefer to settle a good case rather than to have its CEO tied up in a deposition as she is negotiating an important deal. Learning to help inside counsel achieve their legitimate corporate objectives in an economical way is extremely important.

Budgeting is of utmost concern to corporate counsel. So as you move forward in your career, find ways to "partner" with corporate counsel so that costs can be minimized. They need to know not only about the probability of success in any legal matter, but they also need to know about the realistic cost. You will be their hero if you beat your honest cost estimate and achieve a great result.

MARKETING

All law involves marketing. Whether we are trying to convince an opposing party in a business negotiation, a judge in an oral argument, a jury in a trial, or a prospective new client, we are salespeople. Indeed, sales may be the most important aspect of what we do as lawyers.

You may be surprised to learn that as a new lawyer, you will principally be marketing yourself to lawyers in your own firm. They are the main customers for your services. But in the longer run, you will also have to market to the wider community to develop your business. Starting to do this at the earliest possible stage of your career will ensure better results as you move on.

I have spent years marketing myself and my firm. I have seen lawyers who were good at marketing and seemed to succeed effortlessly. I have seen lawyers who failed despite a good deal of effort. But most lawyers are like me. They work hard and ultimately succeed in proportion to their marketing efforts. This brings us to the first rule of marketing: *You must be motivated to sell successfully.*

Several years ago, I attended a seminar given by the Women Rainmakers Committee of the American Bar Association. The panelists included a number of highly successful women rainmakers who were describing their techniques for success. What struck me, however, was not the creativity of their techniques, but the circumstances of their lives. In each case, the panelist had begun marketing efforts when some major—usually negative—circumstance had occurred in her life or practice. For example, one woman suddenly learned that her large firm had failed. At the same time, her marriage also failed. She found herself on her own, without the principal supports upon which she had been relying. She had to market herself aggressively to survive.

The ability to sell with a contagious enthusiasm is, in large part, born of necessity. *Unless you can make yourself believe that marketing is essential to your survival, it is unlikely that you will succeed.* The effort to market is simply too great. Moreover, you cannot convincingly sell yourself unless you believe in yourself and your services.

If you need a little motivation, consider how many lawyers have been recently laid off without warning. Each of them has suddenly found himself or herself in a situation in which marketing is essential. Their ability to secure new employment will be determined in some degree by the networking they have done and perhaps by the business they have generated. Successful marketers always have independence, which is the best security against the changing fortunes of firms.

All marketing is divided into two types. The first involves developing general recognition of your product. It is the type of marketing your firm should be doing to showcase the firm and to create an environment in which individual lawyers can market themselves to clients, who immediately recognize that such lawyers are affiliated with a good firm. As a new lawyer, your participation in this process is generally limited, but you should make an effort to participate in, and to generate ideas for, marketing the firm. For example, you might write an article for the local periodical that will showcase your firm's capabilities. You might suggest that the firm host a cocktail party for an organization with which you have been involved.

The second type of marketing is individual marketing, in which individuals sell themselves and the firm. This type of marketing is largely within your control. It is also the most critical because, to a very high degree, clients hire lawyers rather than firms. So after looking at the latest firm layoffs and convincing yourself that you must do it now, how do you market yourself? The first step is to make a *written plan* of your goals and the specific tasks you will undertake to achieve them. Here are some suggestions I have found helpful to new lawyers.

ANALYZING THE "TARGET MARKET"

At the outset, you have to spend time analyzing your "target market." This starts with the market within your firm and extends out to other markets, including friends and family members, classmates working in corporations and other firms, and personal contacts at companies that can benefit from your firm's expertise.

Do not assume that you have to be an expert in an area of law to sell your firm's expertise. To the contrary, you may make a great deal of headway selling the expertise of others in your firm. If, for example, your firm has a great intellectual property group, you may find that you can sell their services, even if you yourself have no special expertise in the area.

To "cross sell" to the target markets, you have to know what the lawyers in the firm can do. Going hand-in-hand with your analysis of the target market must be an intensive self-education as to the capabilities of the firm.

In analyzing the target market, you should look carefully at the firm's existing clients to see where the firm has had its greatest appeal. Ask for input from more experienced lawyers about the types of clients who have been selecting the firm. Ask your fellow associates about the clients for whom they have worked.

MARKETING WITHIN THE FIRM

The first market to which you should address yourself is the firm itself. To market yourself within the firm, you have to produce good work and get to know all of the lawyers. Constantly find ways to introduce yourself to everyone. If you are low on work, send word (perhaps by e-mail) that you are available to help. Project a positive image. Make many friends. Make no enemies.

Remember that you cannot get the work you want unless the senior lawyers know who you are. They will not typically know you unless they have been working with you or have been introduced to you at least three or four times. So take every opportunity to introduce and reintroduce yourself.

MARKETING OUTSIDE THE FIRM

Outside of the firm, there are numerous opportunities to market yourself and your firm. Everyone has her or his own technique, but all of them are oriented toward the solution of one basic challenge. When a client or a referring lawyer is looking for a lawyer, the person usually has only a few minutes to come up with names. The first name coming to his or her mind should be yours.

Here are a few techniques that tend to work over time, particularly if you stay oriented to your target markets and recognize that you must put your name repeatedly in front of those markets:

a. Develop an e-mail list of your friends and acquaintances. Send them announcements and other materials periodically.

b. *Join and use networks.* Use not only bar networks but also business networks such as trade associations related to your area of law. If you are a woman or minority, use networks of these groups.

c. Keep special track of people in your networks that are in a position to send your firm business. Today technology offers a multitude of ways to do this. E-mail makes it easy to send notes to everyone you know. Facebook enables you to network with your friends and look them up. (I am a little more skeptical about blogs, since careless public statements may harm you.)

d. Meet lawyers and judges in your community. You can do this easily by becoming active in your bar associations. Even if it does not bring you business directly, your familiarity with local lawyers and judges is a valuable asset to market.

e. Follow up your mailings with telephone calls.

f. Learn to introduce yourself in an effective manner that not only conveys your name, but also the specialty of both you and your firm (e.g., "I am Jane Smith, a lawyer with Piggly, Wiggly and Igilly. We specialize in helping companies register and protect their patents and trademarks.").

g. Develop a special expertise, a niche that can be marketed.

h. Provide early reconnaissance to clients about emerging legal issues. Keep a keen eye out for lawsuits that have been filed so that you can see opportunities for your firm to participate. For example, if you see that a client of the firm has become a defendant in an industry-wide lawsuit, you can mobilize the contacts of the firm to see if the firm can inquire about representing the client. Alternatively, there may be ways to mobilize an existing client to intervene in a lawsuit, either as a party or as *amicus curiae.*

DEVELOPING A WRITTEN MARKETING PLAN

Marketing is a lifelong effort. If you do not start the process early in your career, you cannot reap the rewards years later. And while it is true that the most productive years for lawyers are their forties and fifties, the productivity of lawyers in those years is in direct proportion to the effort expended in the early years of their careers.

A written marketing plan is essential and must set specific goals with reasonable time frames for accomplishing them. The written marketing plan will force you to think about your broad career goals and your near-term assignments. Written plans also help you discipline your effort and focus it in a productive way. The plans will also allow you to measure your progress and remember the items on which you need to work.

The plan should include broad career goals (e.g., "I want to make $1 million a year," or "I want to change the system to serve poor people more effectively."). It should also set out specific tasks in different areas, including (a) building your reputation, both inside and outside the firm, (b) developing community activities, (c) continuing education and specialization,

(d) staying in contact with possible referral sources, and, of course, with clients ("networking").

You should also make an inventory of your strengths and weaknesses. Be sure that your plan addresses those strengths and weaknesses. For example, I have always had a mild phobia about calling people. As a result, I have always made a list of old acquaintances to call as part of my plan. This exercise forces me to make the calls and reminds me to do so when I would otherwise conveniently—and perhaps unconsciously—forget. Similarly, I am very good at marketing my firm to lawyers in other firms who want to make a change in their careers. So I also make a list of potential lateral hires to pursue.

The use of a written plan is essential. It is clear that when you write out your goals, you will have a good chance of achieving them, even if you never look at the paper again. The reason is that you have implanted a subconscious suggestion in your mind that will continue to motivate you. Of course, revisiting the plan is always a good idea. You should take some action, however small, every day to achieve each of the goals you have set and evaluate your efforts periodically.

If you would like help in creating a template for your marketing plan, you can use one that is available for free on the Internet at http://www.lfmi.com. Be sure that the plan is detailed. It must include specifics of what you are going to do, whom you are going to contact, and how many hours you are going to work. The more detailed it is, the more effective it will be.

Evaluation of your marketing efforts is not like grading a multiple-choice test. You win even if you "fail." Remember that almost every failure in marketing is simply the elimination of a method that does not work for you. It makes it more likely you will succeed in the future. Do not be afraid to discard things that do not work, although you should be careful not to throw things out without giving them a chance. The fact that your first cocktail party at the bar association did not result in a new case is not a cause for alarm. Do not give up. Your efforts today may only pay off ten years from now, but that payoff can be enormous. *Above all, remember that marketing is a lifelong effort.*

BEGGING, GIVING, CROSS-SELLING, ADVERTISING, BUT NOT THEFT

Beyond general marketing, there are five specific methods of getting business, which I have categorized above and explained below.

1. **Begging.** You can get a lot of business by begging. As humiliating as it may be, it is the best way to get business because it is a direct appeal. People generally want to help others and to receive information about services of which they are unaware. Even if you are told no—and you will be many, many times—remember that "no" is not "no forever," it is just "no, not now." Later everything can, and probably will, change.

2. **Giving.** Often you can attract clients just by giving them something appropriate. I am talking here about modest entertainment of potential clients or providing helpful information to them, such as a synopsis of recent legislative changes or a copy of a complaint that has just been filed against the client. Also included in this category is the payment of *lawful* referral fees, as is customary in contingent fee matters. (Check your state rules of professional conduct.) Of course, you should avoid any gift which is lavish or subject to criticism either because it is illegal or because it is unseemly.

3. **Cross-Selling.** As noted earlier, you can sell your colleagues' expertise. This may seem obvious, but it is difficult and requires careful study of this expertise. (Note that they are not always good marketers of their own expertise, so it may take some effort to catalogue their skills).

4. **Advertising.** There are many forms of advertising, and you must begin by checking your local rules of professional conduct to see what is permissible. Generally you can engage in advertising—commercial speech—that is not misleading. Your latitude with existing clients is greater than with prospective clients. And your latitude to solicit lawyers is greater than it is with soliciting lay people. The rules of all states permit you to give talks and write articles, which are very good methods of advertising.

5. **Theft.** One method of acquiring clients is to steal them from other lawyers. Of course, stealing cases from other attorneys is sometimes unethical. I can remember one lawyer who tried to poach a client from me by falsely telling the client that I had withdrawn from the representation and was no longer representing him.

Even in cases where you acquire a client by referral, you should be careful to respect the fact that the client may still have a relationship with the referring attorney on other matters. Here poaching the client is not only poor form. It is ultimately futile, because referring lawyers avoid client poachers like the plague.

Study the successful attorneys in your firm. Surprisingly, they will generally be willing to help you learn their techniques of marketing. Don't assume that it comes naturally to some people. The reality is that marketing is a learned skill, so you can learn it.

ETHICAL CONSIDERATIONS IN MARKETING

Given what we see in the business and political world, it may seem that ethics and marketing are in tension with each other. Although it was traditionally banned in the legal profession, the modern view is that marketing, within limits, is permissible and necessary. It is commonplace today, and it is expressly allowed under the First Amendment precedents of the Supreme Court of the United States.[41] Moreover, the dissemination of honest information in the marketplace can only benefit consumers by providing them with information with which to select attorneys.

Each state has specific rules on marketing, which you should review and follow. They all begin with a general proscription against false advertising, but they may include more intricate rules about direct solicitation of clients and self-laudatory statements. Many states require prior bar approval of direct solicitation materials. They also tend to be much more lenient with solicitation of existing and prospective clients who have asked you to provide written materials. Rules for Internet Web sites are still evolving, and you have to be aware of the ethical constrictions that may be imposed on your firm's Web site and your Internet postings.

OBTAINING SUPPORT FROM THE FIRM

Marketing by new lawyers is sometimes controversial. Some firms believe that new lawyers should only work in the library, learning the basics of legal practice. In reality, they simply want young lawyers to get their work done and do not appreciate the

---

41. *See*, Bates v. State Bar of Arizona, 433 U.S. 35 (1977) and its progeny.

contribution that these lawyers could make to the firm's overall marketing effort. A law firm is a web of contacts stretching out to grab work. The larger you make the web, the better. It takes only one major case to be developed by an associate to make the whole marketing effort of new lawyers financially worthwhile. And down the road, new lawyers will become more productive rainmakers by initiating efforts early on. So whether you are encouraged to do so or not, be a marketer. Make a business plan and follow it.

The contributions of new lawyers should never be underestimated. I remember speaking to the general counsel of a major Fortune 500 corporation a few years ago, who told me of how his company had come to hire a major law firm. He said that a junior lawyer in the firm had been assigned to handle a relatively simple matter for the company and had done an outstanding job. As a result of this work and the responsiveness of the young lawyer, the company had decided to redirect all of its work to the firm and to use the young lawyer as the principal contact in the firm. Over and over, I have seen this happen. Your efforts will pay off if they are sustained.

You may find that your efforts receive more support in the firm if you show your written plan to one or more of the senior lawyers so that both you and they can be certain that your planned marketing efforts will be helpful to the goals of the firm. (For example, soliciting DUI cases may not fit into a corporate firm's marketing objectives.)

If you receive a chilly response from your firm in the beginning, try implementing your plan. The worst that will happen is that the firm will not accept business you bring in. However, in my experience, most firms appreciate the new business. Even if they are generally reticent about new lawyers becoming involved in marketing, they will come around when you show them the money.

TAKING CONTROL OF YOUR FUTURE

It should be obvious that you can use the planning methods we have discussed in a wider context than marketing. Luck is a major force in everyone's life, but most successful people have achieved success by planning. You may want to have a great family, participate in politics, or develop a successful dot-com. All of these objectives can most reliably be attained if you have a plan. This is particularly true for lawyers, who are easily immersed in the minutia of cases. If you are too absorbed by work, you will not spend enough time thinking about long-term life plans, which can make all the difference to your happiness. As many people will tell you, there are very few lawyers who, at the moment of their death, regret having failed to bill more hours. The potential successes of your career and your life will hopefully go far beyond the confines of your desk. So make a plan and live the plan. You will find that just by writing down your goals, you will program yourself to accomplish them.

The principal prerequisite to successful life planning is making time to do it. Believe it or not, this is also the most serious obstacle. Everyone is so keyed up thinking about the crises of the moment that no planning takes place. After a day of fending off the current crises, there is no time or energy left for thoughtful planning.

This point was driven home to me poignantly during the eight years I spent practicing as a solo practitioner. I made what I thought was a decent living. I was working all the time to do it. I was comfortable, but I was not making enough progress professionally. For years, I thought that planning was too much trouble and that I did not have enough time to advance my career. I spent no time thinking about new frontiers to conquer and began to believe that I had no real incentive to change.

After a while, I became increasingly unhappy with my work. I began to realize that I was too bogged down with administrative matters, and that as an army of one, I could not get the type of cases on which I wanted to work. The frustration grew slowly, but eventually I decided to make some real changes. And to do that, I had to spend a lot of time planning my next move.

I considered applying to the biggest firms in town. I almost went to work for one that ultimately went bankrupt. I considered going to work in another city. I considered going back into government, where I had spent some time. In the end, I decided to go with a small firm. They needed me more than the big guys, and they wanted me to succeed. They also had a desire to grow, and this gave me the idea that I could grow with them.

In the new firm, there was a real desire to build the practice. The partners knew that this effort would require a great deal of time spent planning the growth. Not only did we draw up marketing plans, but we also studied our competitors. We interviewed the survivors of firms that had failed. We tried to see how we could avoid their mistakes and improve on their planning (or lack of it). We created detailed agendas and plans.

Despite enormous odds during a difficult economic time when even the some big firms were having trouble staying afloat, our office went from nineteen lawyers to over 150 lawyers. We became the largest and one of the most successful firms in our city and state. I can assure you that very little of the success was due to luck. We made the time for continuous planning, and the results were astounding.

As a new lawyer, you have an enormous number of options open to you. So planning becomes absolutely essential. If your objective is to become a partner in the firm, you need both a written marketing plan and a written career plan. If it normally takes eight years to become a partner, you should plan the eight years. You should consider how you will become an owner of the firm in that time. You should consider where you need to be each year in terms of professional skill, political success within the organization, community recognition, and business development.

Of course, in life, our planning has to go well beyond the profession of law. We have to meet financial goals. We have to meet personal goals. And here too the only way to succeed is to plan. We need to take time to write down the larger goals and identify steps to take immediately to accomplish them. It is only through this discipline that we can identify what we want to do and enhance our likelihood of success.

So you should sit down and make a list of all of the things you want in life, even if they seem to be beyond what you think you can accomplish. This simple action will set everything in motion.[42] Keep your list close at hand, and every day take some step toward realizing each goal. Revise your goals periodically and evaluate your success. Be prepared to take action to make the goals a reality.

Remember that you can never fail. You may succeed in eliminating unsuccessful strategies, but as long as you keep planning and striving, you will win because you are consciously and unconsciously motivated to win.

---

42. Of course, there is a subset of people who seem to fear success or the envy and other problems success might bring. These people do not succeed and continue to "shoot themselves in the foot." I doubt you are one of them, but if you are, get some professional counseling to overcome it.

UNDERSTANDING LAW FIRM ECONOMICS

Whether you believe it or not, you have embarked upon a business venture when you join a firm. You may be called an associate, but you are very much a partner in the enterprise. So it is important to know some basic things about the economics of firms. In this chapter, we will cover the economic structure of most firms in a way that will help you to be more productive and understand your role more clearly.

Each firm, of course, thinks it is unique. Whatever is said, however, all firms must obey similar economic rules or perish. And the way they obey tends to be relatively consistent, despite a fair amount of rhetoric to the contrary.

TIME IS INVENTORY. RECORD IT!

The inventory of all law firms is time. That means that law firms derive their revenue from time spent on cases. So you would think that spending time on cases would make you a profitable lawyer. But that is far from axiomatic. You can work like a dog and still be unprofitable.

It is common for lawyers to forget to record their time. Sometimes this is due to the press of work. Most commonly, however, it is due to the nuisance it creates. You have worked all day for a client. It is 10:00 p.m. Who wants to spend fifteen minutes finalizing the timesheet? You want to go home and relax. Believe me when I tell you that this spells disaster. As I said earlier, you must keep track of your time as you go through the day. Otherwise you will almost certainly work harder than you need to in order to rise in your firm.

Record your time in tenths of an hour. Anything else is "unit billing" and will be obvious to anyone who reviews your bill. In some jurisdictions it is considered unethical. Keep the record throughout the day. Otherwise you will forget what you did.

Record *all* of your time. Let the firm decide whether you have been efficient. Your comparatively low hourly rate reflects your lack of productivity as a new lawyer. If you start writing off time unilaterally, you are not being faithful to yourself or your firm, to which you are a fiduciary.

Never record more time than you actually spent. It is dishonest and will be relatively obvious to everyone. At best it will lead to write-offs of your time. At worst it will justifiably lead to your dismissal.

A word for those who think they can do their timesheets at the end of the month. You are a detriment to your organization.

It is difficult to believe that you can accurately reconstruct your timesheets, even if you have good notes. No client should receive a bill concocted this way. Consider timesheet procrastination to be a serious disease and treat it aggressively, before your firm or the client treats it for you.

BILLING EARLY AND OFTEN

Time must be converted into money. So billing for your time is a critical factor. If your time is written off because it is excessive or is not billed on a monthly or quarterly basis, you may not be a profitable lawyer, even if you work hard.

Sometimes, when your time is billed, you still may not be profitable. That can occur because of your rate and your "realization." Most firms have a range of rates for lawyers at all levels, which goes up with seniority. In some firms, each lawyer may have several rates, depending upon the type of work or special arrangements with the client. It is worth knowing your rate(s) so that you can begin to appreciate whether you are a profitable lawyer. Simply multiply your rate times the number of billable hours you are working.

That said, even if your time is charged at a high rate, you work hard, *and* you record your time, you still may lose money because the clients do not pay.

COLLECTION

Clients do not pay for several reasons.

1. Lawyers are notoriously slow in sending bills and demanding payment. I have been amazed to see how some lawyers consistently put off the simple mechanics of sending out a bill. It is almost like they are embarrassed to send the bill or they

have some mental block against it. Perhaps it is simply the procrastination syndrome again.

2. Some clients are deadbeats and don't intend to pay. Hopefully your firm is careful to avoid deadbeats in its intake procedures and to obtain retainers that will cover the costs of the services; however, deadbeat clients are a common problem in almost every law firm.

3. Clients do not like to pay lawyers because they think that lawyers are a necessary evil, but not a financial catalyst. They hate the bills and delay paying them.

4. Clients do not pay because they run out of money. In the current economic downturn, we unfortunately see more of this.

Let's assume that you work a lot of hours, record your time faithfully, charge a high rate, and collect the money from clients who recognize the great value of your work. Even then, you still may not be profitable, due to the cost of employing you. So let's talk about the cost structure of a law firm.

COSTS

Law firms, like other businesses, have two kinds of costs: fixed and variable. Broadly speaking, fixed costs are expenses that do not vary based upon the amount of services sold by the firm. Variable costs vary according to the amount of output of the services sold.

Variable costs in a law firm include a portion of telephone service, supplies, and a host of other elements of running a firm that are related to the number of billable hours the firm produces. In a month when billable hours are light, these expenses are also light.

Unfortunately, most of the costs of a law firm are fixed. The fixed cost of a law firm includes its rent and the cost of loans taken out to buy capital items such as office renovations, furniture, equipment, and library books. So if your office is the Taj Mahal, the chances are that the fixed cost is very high. Moreover, the cost of a new lawyer is essentially the same with respect to these particular fixed costs as that of an experienced lawyer.

The most significant item of fixed cost in law firms is the cost of lawyers' salaries, which must be paid whether the billable hours are high in a given month or not. So as proud as you are of your starting megabucks salary, remember that, economically, your salary is a drag on your profitability. Sorry to put a black cloud around your silver lining!

Salary cost is an issue that is particularly significant at the current moment. In 2000, firms across the United States were forced to raise salaries for associates to compete with opportunities for lawyers available servicing the burgeoning computer industry. After the computer bubble burst, salaries did not come down—at least not at the high salary end of the associate market. Additionally, real estate and other costs have escalated in the period since 2000. Obviously this has put substantial pressure on firms to raise rates at a moment when the economy is in the midst of a "hard landing." If the firms have to absorb some of the cost—and they probably will—the profitability of associates will be undermined. It is far from a perfect scenario. However, your awareness of it is essential and may lead you to creative opportunities for enhancing efficiency.

Notice that as businesses with a large fixed costs and relatively low variable costs, law firms must have substantial and relatively continuous revenue to avoid losing money. However, when the revenue surpasses the fixed costs, a great percentage of that additional revenue is pure profit because variable costs associated with increased output do not eat up the revenue. Thus, in good years, the partners can profit greatly. In bad years, fixed costs can result quite suddenly in substantial reductions in profit and even losses. That threat looms in times of economic recession.

MARGINAL VS. FULL COST

The cost of carrying a lawyer is at least $100,000–$250,000 *before* salary. I measure this on what is known as a "full cost" basis. This method essentially involves taking the total annual costs of the firm, other than attorney salaries, and dividing it by the total number of lawyers. In reality, the "marginal cost" of adding one lawyer may be less because that one lawyer can utilize some of the existing internal services of the firm, such as the accounting department, the library, the computer mainframes, the phones, and underutilized space.

Unfortunately, many firms attempt to operate as if the marginal cost were the real cost. When they do this, they are surprised to find that the cost is really higher than they budgeted. At certain points in the spectrum of growth, adding an extra lawyer means adding a new floor of space, a new accounting system, a new set of non-professional staff, etc. At these points, the marginal cost of adding one attorney rises quite dramatically—and sometimes unexpectedly.

FISCAL YEAR: THE DAY OF RECKONING

Always bear in mind the concept of the fiscal year. This is the point at which the IRS, at least, requires measurement.

It is at this point that the budget created at the beginning of the year is measured against performance. As the date approaches, the firm scurries around trying to get the clients to pay. Your profitability turns on the success of the firm in meeting its budget projections. For partners and shareholders whose income is in part deferred until the last day of the year, the process of year-end collection is critical to getting paid.

One way law firms differ from normal businesses is that at the end of the fiscal year, they usually distribute all of their profit to their owners. The reasons for this are many. Some are historical. Firms were small groups of lawyers who were accustomed to dividing the pie at the end of the year. The idea of a megafirm with an institutional life of its own was unknown.

Some reasons for year-end distribution involve taxation. If the firm is a corporation, it has to distribute its income to its shareholder-employees at the end of the year to avoid double taxation at the corporate and shareholder levels. Similarly, partners in a law firm partnership are taxed on the income of the firm, whether or not it is distributed. If there is no distribution, there is no money to pay the tax. This might seem insignificant to you, but I can assure you that, as we will see in a moment, it means everything.

CAPITAL

Capital is an absolutely critical and central aspect of law firm economics, yet it is a mystery to most lawyers, including members of law firms. Let's demystify it!

Every firm needs capital invested by its shareholders or partners. (Let's call them the "owners.") And although some firms will tell you otherwise, the need for capital is immutable. A firm needs capital investment to pay for furniture, computers, and most importantly, to pay employees (including you). Working capital for salaries is particularly essential in the early part of the fiscal year, when the cash of the firm has been depleted by year-end distributions and when new money has not yet been collected from clients.

There is also a less obvious reason that law firms need capital. As noted earlier, law firms typically distribute all of their income to the owners at the end of the fiscal year. Some of the firm's expenditures are not tax deductible (e.g., capital expenditures, which must be depreciated over time, social club dues, and some meal expenses). The firm shells out real money for these costs during the year, but it gets no deduction. Therefore, at the end of the year, the firm is left with income on which taxes are due. Unfortunately, the firm has already shelled out its cash for these nondeductible items. So the firm has to raise cash either to pay its taxes or "zero out" income at the corporate level by giving a deductible salary to the owners. There are only two alternatives to raising the cash: the owners must invest or the firm must borrow from a bank.

It may shock you to learn that the permanent capital cost of a lawyer in an average firm is at the very least between $15,000 and $50,000.[43] This includes not only the year-end tax issue, but also the obvious items, such as a personal computer, furniture, the build-out of an office, and even additional library facilities. To that amount, you must add the cost of working capital to carry the new lawyer during the first several months after he or she starts work, when he or she is working, but no money has been received for that work.

---

43. James D. Cotterman, *Capitalization, Debt, and Taxes*, ALTMAN WEIL REPORT TO LEGAL MANAGEMENT, June 2000.

Firms have developed a variety of ways to deal with the capital problem. You will find it helpful to know what they are so that you can understand the types of problems with which the owners must cope. Most firms require the owners to invest capital. (And you thought that becoming a partner was such a good deal!) Additionally, most firms augment this investment by deferring a portion of the pay of at least the most highly compensated owners until the end of the fiscal year. This deferral means that the owners receive a "draw," which is less than their projected salary through the year. If by the end of the year the money materializes, they get paid. During the year, their deferred compensation acts as working capital available to pay expenses, including your salary.

Another method of dealing with capital is for the firm or its owners—or both—to borrow money, either by borrowing outright from banks or by leasing capital items. This includes leases on built-out space. Since lenders and lessors often insist on full personal recourse against the owners on such borrowing,[44] this is really a thinly disguised and initially painless way of forcing the owners to pay in the capital.[45]

Firms vary in the methods by which they raise capital, but they all raise it. Some hide the capital contribution by borrowing or leasing. Some demand that the new partner put up a great deal of money. Some arrange with a bank to provide loans to partners to put up capital. Some let partners pay in by with-

---

44. In a general partnership, of course, the partners have individual liability for partnership debts.

45. In severe cases, where there is not enough cash at the end of the year to pay owners their projected salary and bonuses, the firm management may resort to "painless" borrowing to cover up the problem. In firms where such borrowing occurs, the results are usually catastrophic.

holding it from their bonus in yearly installments. *But all firms require owners of the firms to pay capital at some point.*

You might think that the issue of capital is a remote problem for an associate, one that will arise many years down the road. Unfortunately, in an economic downturn, issues of capital are critical to everyone who works in the firm. If the firm's owners have invested enough capital, the firm can weather a slowdown in receipts and avoid layoffs, at least to a degree. If, however, the firm has borrowed heavily, the failure in any month to receive payment from clients can lead to an immediate default on the loans. This results in acceleration of the loans, calls on the owners' guarantees, and the consequent failure of the firm. Often a failure can take place in a few days or weeks. Once the word leaks out that the firm is in trouble, the lawyers in the firm look for other jobs, and the firm must shut down to avoid hemorrhaging cash.[46] Clients stop paying outstanding bills once the firm stops representing them. The result is then bankruptcy.

So how do you know how well your firm is capitalized? The short and scary answer is that *almost no firm is sufficiently capitalized.* When you walk into the lavish offices of the great firms, you are impressed with their apparent solidity and endurance. Space abounds. There is oak paneling on the walls. The lighting is exquisite. There are oil paintings of long-deceased firm

---

46. Indeed, many bank loan agreements with law firms have covenants that allow the bank to accelerate the loans when a certain percentage of equity partners leave. The triggering of such a covenant was the direct cause of the failure of Heller Ehrman, a well-respected and successful San Francisco firm that went into bankruptcy two years after it enjoyed its most profitable year ever. *See, Recession Batters Law Firms, Triggering Layoffs, Closings*, THE WALL STREET JOURNAL, January 26, 2009.

leaders. It all looks impervious to the vicissitudes of economic life. Unfortunately, all of the space is leased. The computers and copiers are usually leased. And even though the owners think they have paid in so much capital that everything must be fine, they are usually wrong. They typically forget that, even if they have controlled the amount of the firm's debt, the office leases constitute an enormous liability against which their capital pales in comparison. If revenues fall, the copiers will be repossessed and the firm evicted from its beautiful space.

When you look at the firm failures that have occurred, many of the firms have been large old-line firms with apparently impeccable credentials. Longevity is no protection. Size is no guarantee of capital stability. And in a world where many firms have used borrowing to avoid painful decisions about spending money, one must assume the possibility of difficulties in any firm.

So however much you love your firm—and I sincerely hope you do—you always have to have an exit strategy if the firm folds. And know that even if you work hard, your time is faithfully recorded and billed, the clients pay, and the firm controls costs, you may still find that you are not in a profitable business. I suggest you always keep this in mind as a motivation for all of your marketing and self-improvement efforts. Your survival depends on it—no matter how solid the wood on the walls of the firm.

THE UNEASY CASE FOR HIRING NEW LAWYERS

If it is so expensive, why do firms hire new lawyers? The answer basically turns either on projections of profitability or on myths. In the world of business, the survivors are good at projections of profitability. In the world of law firm management, however, it is often myths that prevail.

At most responsible firms, before the beginning of the fiscal year, the managers engage in a process of carefully budgeting projected revenues and expenses. This is not, as you might expect, primarily done on the basis of predictions about business trends. Usually it is done by taking the past year's costs and revenues and cranking them up an arbitrary percentage.[47] This, of course, is quite scary because it involves only a rough estimate of demand in the marketplace for the firm's services.[48] Still, it is better than no budget, and hopefully it errs on the conservative side in firms that have had growing business.

Once the budget is prepared, it becomes "clear" that new lawyers are needed to cope with increasing workloads. This becomes even more obvious when one realizes that the average trial lawyer in the United States works more than fifty hours per week. If a client comes in with a new case, how can the case be handled? Additionally, there is further pressure from attrition in firms as lawyers leave for one reason or another. Replacement is therefore inevitable.

At some firms, there is a view that hiring of associates increases profit because it increases "leverage." The sad fact, however, is that, for most firms, leverage is an elusive goal. New lawyers are expensive. They drain resources immediately, but do not produce revenues immediately. They are often inefficient, which leads to substantial write-offs of their time. The result is that most firms lose money on new lawyers and

---

47.   Of course, at the present moment, firms are doing precisely the opposite out of fear of the recession. However, they will likely revert to the old methods as soon as the economy turns around.

48.   Recently, of course, we have seen the tragic consequences of the inability of firms to budget revenues in difficult economic times.

barely break even on them after two or three years. Moreover, it is usually far more efficient to take associates with two of three years' experience and improve their productivity than it is to hire inexperienced lawyers and train them to be productive.

My review of the two hundred largest firms in the United States, as identified by *The American Lawyer*, shows absolutely no relationship between leverage (the equity partner to total lawyer ratio) and profitability. Some profitable firms make money with associates. Some do not. This is an area, therefore, where firms may justifiably claim that their economics are unique. In the final analysis, hiring new lawyers becomes an imperative for most law firms, but the degree to which the firm can profit from such hiring varies. This variance has a real impact on salaries, work environment, and, ultimately, partnership opportunities.

In the current environment, where economic visibility is lacking, firms that have a lot of bank debt will not hesitate to lay off lawyers. Significantly, out of the five most highly leveraged firms in the Am Law 100, three have announced layoffs and one has dissolved.[49] The reality for most clients is that having more lawyers working on a case does not improve productivity; it compounds the bills. One general counsel was recently quoted as saying, "I don't have a problem with a $1,000-an-hour lawyer, but the $350-an-hour junior associate isn't worth it."[50]

---

49.   Susan Beck, *Work Like an Egyptian*, NEW YORK LAWYER, January 29, 2009.

50.   *Id.*

MEASURING ECONOMIC PERFORMANCE

So now we know that if you work hard, you record your time, your time is billed promptly, the clients pay, the expenses of the firm are properly budgeted and controlled, and the firm is properly capitalized, you can be a profitable lawyer. But how is all this measured? The answer, of course, is that not all firms measure profitability correctly. If it is not correctly measured, it may mean that you can survive without being profitable for a while, but not forever. Hopefully firms measure performance on a monthly, quarterly, and yearly basis. This enables the firm to get on top of problems before they get out of hand.

The difficulty for the new lawyer, however, is that most firms obscure from their associates the data from which they can judge their economic performance. In a firm where everything is running smoothly, this lack of transparency presents no real problem. However, almost all firms have difficult times. Your job can be jeopardized by forces about which you have no knowledge and over which you consequently have no control. It is therefore important to ask for the information so that you can keep yourself working hard on profitable work, which pays the firm a good return on your labor. You ultimately want to be an owner rather than an employee. Begin acting like an owner by tactfully asking the managing partner for at least some of the data you need to judge your own profitability.

LAW FIRM ORGANIZATION

A natural corollary to the issue of law firm economics is the issue of law firm organization. How are firms really organized? Does it have implications for you, your profitability, and your salary? The short answer is that firms are organized in different ways and that organization seems to have no consistent relationship to profitability or even stability.

THE ECONOMIC ELITE

Law firms are generally governed by those who have economic influence, whatever the formal structure of the firm may be. It is hard for a firm to say no to a partner who controls millions of dollars in business unless there is something inappropriate about the business or the way it is handled.

Some lawyers with economic power choose to govern indirectly by leaving administrative matters to their lieutenants. Other lawyers feel that they need the formal titles that come with administrative positions. Since a lawyer cannot be an outstanding developer of business if he or she spends time exclusively on administrative issues, my experience is that many successful firm leaders often have no formal administrative title.

Rainmakers are leaders—not only because they bring in money, but also because they tend to project a positive influence. They are generally more optimistic and more driven. They are the principal spokespersons for the firm in the outside world. And it follows that their leadership is felt within the firm, where they are also often spokespersons for the organizational cause as well as their individual interests.

OPEN VS. CLOSED SYSTEMS

Where law firms typically differ is in the openness of firm governance. Here there are two styles with various hybrids. Open systems involve boards of directors, the meetings of which are open in some way to members of the firm. In open systems, the compensation of each member and the basis of the compensation are disclosed to all. Closed systems involve a small group, or even one member, who decides everything for everyone. In closed systems, compensation is generally secret, and members are often sworn to secrecy about their own compensation.

As I said at the outset, I have not been able to discern any correlation between the economic success of firms and their organization. Each method of organization has benefits. In a democratic system, there is usually confidence in the compensation and governance system based upon the belief (and sometimes the fact) that there is no way to hide injustice as between the members. In a closed system, however, there is flexibility to reward members of the team whose contributions may be less tangible in any given year. Every firm needs specialists of one sort or another. These specialists may not be economically productive, but they are indispensable to the operation. Such specialists generally cannot be compensated as well in an open system.

Each type of system develops its own problems in the long term. In closed systems, there is an opportunity for members of the "ruling clique" to allocate excessive compensation and perks to themselves. If this problem occurs, it exacerbates suspicion and envy, which are endemic in all law firms.

I think open systems have tremendous institutional benefits because they foster confidence. This is particularly true for potential lateral hires, who come into a firm with some assurance that they will have access to information that will enable them to participate in firm decisions. However, open systems also tend to waste a lot of energy. Compensation debates become endless searches for the "truth." Recruiting new partners and associates becomes one long committee meeting, sapping the reserves of even the most efficient firms and dedicated partners.

The firms that really succeed are able to shift their organizational structures, at least incrementally, in response to changing size and other dynamics. While the firm is smaller, they tend to be more open. As they get bigger, there is less democracy, although they can still be inclusive and representative through well-organized governance structures.

COMPENSATION METHODS

Firms have a wide variety of compensation methods although in the end economic realities generally control the process over time. Some firms pay each partner strictly by seniority. This "lock step" system tends to reward longevity; however, it leads to bitterness over supporting partners who are no longer productive. Successful firms with this model generally select partners very carefully to ensure both compatibility and productivity. Only the neurotically driven need apply! Further, these systems tend to encourage partners to retire earlier so that there is no slacking off on productivity.

Other firms pay varying amounts to partners based, at least in part, on productivity. At the extreme end of the spectrum, these firms are sometimes characterized as "eat what you kill" firms. While these firms tend to select hard workers who are economic dynamos, they tend to suffer from an emphasis on productivity over quality and institutional cohesion.

Although much is made of the different methods of compensation, I believe that over time, all firms must reward partners on an objective basis or lose them. Successful firms rarely benefit by losing productive partners. Therefore, over time, the results of the compensation systems of successful firms tend to converge. Furthermore, high quality tends to lead to better economic productivity.

One factor that enters into the compensation equation is the degree to which the firm generates business for its owners.[51] In some of the leading law firms, the firm's name has sufficient goodwill that it produces cases and matters for lawyers. In this situation, the business-getting prowess of the owners plays a less important role in determining compensation. In contrast, in other firms, the firm provides a "platform" from which the individual owners can use their abilities to acquire business. In this

---

51.   Professors Gilson and Mnookin have referred to this phenomenon as "firm specific capital." Ronald J. Gilson and Robert H. Mnookin, *Sharing Among the Human Capitalists: An Economic Inquiry into the Corporate Law Firm and How Partners Split Profits*, 37 STAN. L. REV. 314 (1984–1985).

situation, compensation tends to be based in greater measure on the individual business acquisition effort of each lawyer.

EQUITY VS. NON-EQUITY PARTNERS

Many firms maintain two classes of partners: equity and non-equity partners. Equity partners are owners of the firm who divide its profits. Non-equity partners generally receive guaranteed incomes plus bonuses. Equity partners generally have "tenure." Non-equity partners may be fired at will. Equity partners invest capital; non-equity partners do not.

There are multiple reasons for two-tiered firms. First, firms want to postpone final partnership decisions, particularly in the case of lawyers who are competent journeymen but have no independent book of business. By promoting associates to non-equity partnership status, the firm can hold onto good lawyers and give them more time to develop their business. Second, firms want to increase their *"profits per equity partner."* This is an arbitrary economic metric created by *The American Lawyer* to compare firms. A higher profit per equity partner makes the firm more attractive to lateral partner hires and merger candidates. Promoting associates into a non-equity partnership position avoids the dilution of profits per equity partner. Third, firms that have a two-tiered structure often have some equity partners who skim profit from the firm at the expense of their more productive colleagues. This process is best accomplished when the "victims" have no tenure.

If you sense that I do not think the equity/non-equity structure makes much economic sense, you are right.[52] Theoretically

---

52. Empirical study has shown that there is no economic benefit to a two-tiered system. William D. Henderson, *An Empirical Study of Single-Tier versus Two-Tier Partnerships in the AM LAW 200,*, 84 N.C. LAW. REV 1691 (2005–2006).

a firm should want to increase capital investment by its partners. The two-tier system discourages this. As for the profits-per-equity-partner metric of *The American Lawyer*, it is useless because it can be so easily manipulated, either by reducing the number of equity partners or by simply lying to *The American Lawyer* magazine, a misdeed for which there is no known penalty.

From a political point of view, however, a two-tier system may make some sense. It retains good lawyers to service clients. And in the best firms, the non-equity partners have a leg up in moving to other legal positions outside the firm from which they can send business to the firm. For example, it may be much easier for a corporation to hire as its general counsel a non-equity "partner" at Firm A than an equally qualified "associate" from Firm B.

The empirical evidence suggests that two-tiered firms have no more financial success than single-tiered firms.[53] At a point in our economic lives where there is greater and greater financial pressure on firms, the argument for increasing equity capital by eliminating non-equity tiers is compelling.

CONCENTRATION OF POWER

Firms tend to vary in terms of the concentration of power. Some firms are truly democratic. In these firms, all partners are consulted about significant decisions. Other firms have power concentrated to a very high degree in a few individuals.

Once again the type of organization has an impact on the younger lawyers. In firms with over-concentrations of power, it is essential to become friends with members of the "inner sanctum" to further your career in the firm. Over-concentration of power also tends to create inherent instability. The firm may be run well

53. *Id.*

by a benevolent dictator, but the unwillingness to share power leads to situations in which the firm has no middle-level cadre of managers. Thus the firm is placed in jeopardy when the dictator dies, retires, or loses momentum. Additionally, the economic decisions of one person, unrestrained by informed debate, may either be good or bad; but if they are bad, they are often fatal.

ACCESS TO INFORMATION

For those seeking to become partners, a clear understanding of the firm's organization and economics is obviously essential to ensuring winning performance in the organization. Indeed, it may be quite valuable in choosing a firm in the first place. Unfortunately, most firms think it is in their interest to keep associates uninformed about firm economics. I have yet to fathom why. The more information firms can give to associates about the goals of the firm and the more measurements firms provide of their associates' achievements with respect to these goals, the more likely it becomes that the associates will perform well. Indeed, a totally transparent system in which associates receive complete economic information about themselves and their cohorts should lead to maximum internal motivation and peer pressure to accomplish the firm's goals.

Some firms hide information because they do not want their competitors to be able to "raid" the firm and steal the most profitable attorneys. Some firms hide information from the associates in order to camouflage the lack of productivity of the partners. Some firms fear that information will give the associates too much power. Some simply lack an understanding of the value and power of the information.

There are pros and cons to disclosure, and there is such a thing as too much disclosure to too many people, with too few tools to analyze the data disclosed. However, I believe that access by all lawyers to some reasonable amount of information on their productivity and those of their peers is a successful strategy for any legal organization. Publicly traded companies have provided mounds of information to the public for years without suffering terrible consequences. On balance, the same holds true for law firms.

FIRM CULTURE

It is helpful to be aware of three other important "cultural" dimensions of law firms: positive orientation, risk preference, and attitude toward growth.

By positive culture, I mean the degree to which the organization positively motivates the partners and the employees. Does the firm overcome the normally negative influences of envy and greed? Does the firm cheer on members who achieve? Or are the members of the firm secretly unhappy when someone succeeds? Is the firm a hotbed of intrigue, bearing testimonial to the maxim that the infighting is greatest when the stakes are the lowest?

My experience has been that law firms are often more "negatively charged" places than other businesses for reasons that may have to do with intense individual competition fostered by law schools[54] and a lack of understanding that the entire firm is enhanced by achievements of each member. Firms that are negatively charged constantly degrade their lawyers in subtle and not so subtle ways. They tend to motivate by using fear, rather than commitment, and reward with money, rather than personal recognition.

---

54. *See,* Seligman et al., *supra* note 1.

The truly successful firms are optimistic places that make every lawyer (and client) feel important and needed. They reward with praise as well as money and steadfastly support their lawyers in adversity. The owners feel bound together by personal ties and want to keep practicing together. By contrast, failing firms revel in negativity, compounding their downward spirals.

Risk aversion is another significant organizational dimension. Most large firms punish their members for taking business risks. This arises from the absolute imperative of achieving the annual budget projections of the firm. Firms that are the most successful, however, reward those who take reasonable entrepreneurial risk. Indeed, it has been well known that small plaintiffs' personal injury firms, which have traditionally worked on a contingent fee basis, have been generally more successful economically than firms that work solely on a billable hour basis. There is more entrepreneurial risk in the small personal injury firm, and there is consequently more opportunity for financial reward if things go well.

Yet another dimension of firm culture is the attitude of the firm toward growth. Many firms prize their tightly knit groups of partners and do not seek to grow either in size or geographical location. Yet others seek to follow the model of the accounting firms with their explosive global growth strategies. I tend to think that whatever the downsides—and there are many— firms will continue to grow in size to obtain better work from a wider network of clients and to diversify their market risks.

From the point of view of a new lawyer, the positive orientation of the firm will directly impact the quality of the work environment as well as the long-term prospects of partnership. It is usually easier to work and to develop in a positive environment. Risk aversion may also express itself in ways that are unpleasant. More time may be spent on blaming lawyers for lost cases and other failures than on motivating these lawyers to become more successful in the future.

Finally, be wary of being too judgmental about law firm organizational structures. Good firms pattern themselves in different ways. You can be a superstar in most of them if you learn the dynamics of the organization (i.e., how to use the rules of the game to your advantage). Remember, no organization is perfect, and because of its proximity, your own firm will usually seem less perfect than most.

BUILDING CONSTRUCTIVE RELATIONSHIPS WITHIN THE FIRM

The organizations with which you are affiliated as a lawyer offer rich opportunities to build lasting professional and social relationships. The friendships you make in your work as a new lawyer can be among the most enduring and fulfilling of your life. Your opportunity to develop these relationships is one of the richest treasures of your career. You should pursue this opportunity with passion.

Obviously you will not be loved and admired by everyone, nor do I think this should be the principal goal of any professional. Nevertheless, no organization can function if everyone is an island; therefore, learning the techniques of harmonizing with a group is important. It is not surprising that law firm leaders view interpersonal skills as very important to the success of associates.[55]

In more than thirty years in law, I have seen the social structure of law firms change considerably. Lawyers used to be recruited out of law school in large measure on the basis of their perceived social compatibility. Women were generally excluded from the major law firms. Jews and Catholics set up their own segregated shops. "Blue bloods" dominated the large firms. Lawyers generally stayed in the firms into which they were first inducted. In this world, colleagues were more like members of a clan, and it was difficult and unpleasant to leave the clan.

Today the social fabric of law firms is much more tenuous. Lawyers are more readily hired on the basis of merit. Minority hiring is generally thought of as a responsible aspect of running the business, and clients (particularly large retail clients) often insist on it. Law firms are now in competition for talented people with corporations and accounting firms. Law firms generally have less inherent economic strength because of their high fixed costs and lack of access to capital.

As a result of all of this change, lawyers tend to have the attitude that they can easily leave the firm whenever they want. Even large firms often close down, and fewer lawyers think they will be practicing with the same firm forever. Indeed, in response to the pressures of the practice and the firm, lawyers are always tempted to jump ship.

What is forgotten in all this, of course, is the tremendous investment, personal and economic, which lawyers have made in the firm just by their tenure there and the fact that a move is costly. You have to make new friends and prove yourself all over

---

55.   VAULT, VIEW FROM THE TOP: LAW FIRM LEADERS (Vault Library, 2005).

again. Clients will be lost in the move. Your productivity is reduced (as much as one-third initially) just by the move itself.

So it serves everyone's interests to make things work.
Building solid personal relationships with everyone in the firm
is an ideal for which you should strive. But in a world where the
fabric of the firm is so tenuous, it is not easy to attain.

In any organization, the greatest challenges to interpersonal cohesion are fear and envy. You, of course, will always have
some fear because you are new. But others in the firm may fear
you as well. You may be competition. Your youth may be a
challenge to older lawyers. You may also envy others who appear to be more skilled or successful. Here are a few things to
bear in mind about fear and envy.

When dealing with your own fear, the most important thing
to remember is that even though you are new, you can always
do better if you appear outwardly calm in the face of challenge.
If you use your fear to do better work for your clients rather
than to torture yourself or others, you will succeed. Remember,
you are qualified to do excellent work. It may simply take you
a little longer to get it done.

Envy is a greater challenge. The essence of it is the perception, however fantastic, that someone you envy possesses "magi-
cal" power to succeed, and that you cannot achieve such success.
Please remember that this is a perception and not a reality. To
diffuse your own envy, use the techniques you have learned in
this book to achieve that which you envy. To diffuse the envy
of others, always avoid bragging and help others achieve for
themselves that which you have achieved. Give everyone a pep
talk and try to give him or her tools to succeed.

I also think it is important, as a new lawyer, to listen to and
learn about every person in the firm. Get to know her or his

skills, specialties, and background. Try to find things you can admire about each one. This includes not only lawyers in your office, but in branch offices as well. There are no evil people. There are people who may not support you in different ways from time to time, but if you look more positively at how you can build relationships with everyone, you will be more successful.

Competition with other associates merits some discussion here. It is true that you are theoretically in competition with other associates to become a partner. But there is only a grain of the truth to this theory. If the firm were bigger, the financial pie bigger, and the firm's momentum greater, there would be no competition. There would be sufficient opportunity for most everyone. So it is best to ignore the competitive aspects of your relationship to other associates and help each of them realize his or her own true potential. If you build your colleagues up, you will have more in the end than if you tear them down.

Focus your energy on encouraging your colleagues. Share your research and experience with them. If you see a significant new case, send an e-mail about it to everyone who might be interested. Volunteer to organize continuing legal education and firm events. If you build teams, invite others to join. Leave no one behind. Always remember, this is your firm. You want it to be the best. Take the competition to your adversaries, not your colleagues.

Keep in mind that your fellow associates are just as fragile as you are. They have egos. They like to be praised. So look for things to praise. Tell them how good they look, how smart they were to win a motion, or how happy you are that they have gotten a raise. Tell them how happy you are at the firm. Keep all of your negative thoughts to yourself; if it is necessary to express disapproval of the firm, do it in a positive way. For example, suppose the firm failed to raise the associates' pay in response to the market. If another associate starts complaining about it at lunch, your best response would be, "the firm has generally kept pace with the market. If we bring the relevant data to the attention of management and look for ways to improve our profitability and efficiency, I'm certain we can get the raise within a reasonable period of time."

When you are down, it is hard to build good relationships. So no matter how low you feel, put it out of your mind when you deal with other people. They can only take so much of your griping. I suggest that you focus on positive images before speaking with others. Have positive pictures on your walls. Force yourself to smile, even through the tears. You will not be down for long,[56] and you will raise everyone's spirits. Don't worry; be happy!

Without slighting your goal of building ties to everyone, try to forge especially good relationships with those with whom you work most closely. You will never advance very far if your immediate supervisors despise you. Learn the pecking order enough to peck the right people. Do not worry about others paying you enough respect. Respect is earned; within very broad limits, it cannot be demanded.

Remember, too, that everyone is likely at some point to let you down, leave you in an angry mood, and undermine your efforts. Accept them anyway. It is better to work on improving your dialogue than to cast people away or to constantly search for new friends. We are all human, and all organizations of humans will let you down to some degree. Do not despair. Use balms rather than bombs to repair the damage.

---

56. If you are down for too long, seek professional help. There is no reason to suffer.

DEALING WITH
THE FIRM

BUTTERING UP THE BOSS

Nothing succeeds as well as flattery, as long as it is not too transparent. So think of ways that you can be helpful to the people who employ you and praise them appropriately for their achievements. Offer to do things they are unable or unwilling to do. Nevertheless, beware of the lawyer that craves praise too much. There is a limit to what a lawyer can teach you if the lawyer is really seeking a captive audience of sycophants. There is also a limit to your value if you are nothing more than a sycophant.

Help the senior lawyers to be better people and better lawyers. When they do a good job, tell them. If you see things they could do better, tactfully offer to help them implement some changes. In the last analysis, however, you should always remember that the objective is to help clients achieve *their* goals and not just to help you or your senior lawyer accomplish your goals.

In meetings, it is extremely important not to undermine your colleagues. If you have a point you think they have missed, pass them notes or speak to them privately. Do not contradict them publicly, because it reflects disunity and lack of preparation. A team approach to meetings will lead to a more effective outcome.

These days it is rare for associates to invite partners to dinner or even lunch. It is, however, a good way to get to know the boss in a more informal context and may lead to your being treated in a more humane way. Most firms wisely set up functions to accomplish this, but you can always suggest lunch to someone with whom you are working.

I do not suggest that personal outreach to senior lawyers ought to be overdone, but I do think you can gain something by trying to get to know a kinder, gentler side of the people for whom you work.

HANDLING COMPENSATION AND REVIEWS

There are few things more frightening to a new lawyer than to be "reviewed." Firms have a wide variety of methods for reviewing associates. Most have an annual process tied to compensation. Others have informal reviews that come without warning. You should look at the process as a constructive one. Whatever you are told, it will probably contain some feedback on your performance that you can use.

In preparing for a review, many firms will give you an opportunity to have input. You should keep a good record of your projects so you can provide a list of assignments and the names of the lawyers for whom you have worked. This will enable the reviewing committee to contact as many sources of information as possible. The ideal sources are persons for whom you have done the most work. They must be reasonably happy about your performance or they would not have given you more work.

Be sure you have a good understanding of your statistical performance. At least have a command of your billable hours, fee receipts (if you can get the number), and any pro bono work. You want to be able to sell yourself realistically to the reviewers. Having too low an opinion of yourself is a poor reflection on your skills as an advocate. Having too high an opinion of yourself reflects unrealistic arrogance. A balance is required.

When you receive your review, try to take notes so that you can be sure you understand afterward what was said. Do not become discouraged at suggestions for improvement. These are opportunities for you to do better. You should, therefore, be certain of what is being said. Ask questions and seek clarification if necessary. Remember, you will be missing out on helpful guidance that can lead to your growth as a lawyer if you don't listen carefully.

When discussing your compensation, ask how your compensation stacks up against others in your class. It may hurt to learn that others are making more, but learning it from your cohorts will be far more painful. Ask why you are making less or more, and this information will give you further insight. Ask if you are on track to become a partner and learn more about how the firm views your long-term prospects.

No matter what answer you receive to these pointed questions, do not shoot the messenger. This is a time to listen, not a time to debate. You should remember that a poor review often precedes a good one for those who listen and make efforts to deal with the issues. Even if it is a totally negative review, it will give you the motivation to examine your circumstances and perhaps find more compatible employment. Know that if you got through law school and still have a pulse, you can turn yourself into a great lawyer—if you have the right incentives, the right attitude, and the right method of attack.

Unless you are told otherwise, do not be overly concerned about salary differentials. In firms that do not lock-step associate salaries by class, the decision to pay associates is often made on arbitrary grounds that have to do with economic issues over which the associates have very little control. There is always a tendency to overrate the differences. You should instead focus on the things that can improve your salary. Skill, efficiency, and business generation all contribute to the real goal of compensation, which is to make the money you want and deserve.

If you find that others are making more money and you feel wronged that they are getting more, do not give in to all of the usual negative thoughts: "I have been [bleeped]." "That associate is not worth more than I." "They don't love me." "I was screwed by the committee because..." Try to focus instead on the fact that if someone is currently being paid more when you know him or her to be worth less, you will have a great argument for a raise the next time around. Those who make more and are worth less are actually the "golden geese" that may help you improve your situation in the next round of compensation reviews. Conversely, don't forget that if you are at the top of the salary pyramid, you may be held to a higher standard and face more scrutiny in the future.

Frequently both associates and partners lose their tempers over a few thousand dollars or a poor review. The most unfortunate response is to present the firm with an ultimatum. "If you do not pay me X dollars, I will quit." All institutions have built-in reactions to ultimatums. Sometimes they work, but most of the time they do not. If your bluff is called, you may find yourself out of a job on someone else's terms rather than your own.

The issue for each lawyer in a firm is to find a level of compensation that is reasonable, given his or her legal and economic contribution. Be sure to keep a positive mental attitude toward the process and know that sometimes there will be bumps in the road. Your ability to deal effectively and diplomatically with authority figures will enhance your situation. It is fair to point out an obvious injustice, but it has to be done in a polite way. You will make mistakes, and so will your firm, but they can be rectified. Your ability to cope is a test of your maturity. In the end, you can always quit, but you should only do so on your own terms and after making every reasonable effort to work things out.

DEALING WITH INSTITUTIONAL DOUBLE CROSS

All organizations will cheat you one day. You will fail to get something you want and deserve. You may work for years to become a partner only to be told to wait an additional year. You may not get the raise you want. You may not get a new laptop computer. The list is endless. I urge you to act with the greatest restraint for a number of good reasons.

1. You never want to take action that may be disproportionate to the grievance. Let the matter simmer a bit. Your first reactions tend to be too emotional. With a bit of time, you will gain perspective and the power to deal with the issue most effectively.

Keep in mind the mantra of one of the most skilled government lawyers I ever met. When it came to office politics, he would always say, "I don't care. It doesn't matter." Of course he cared, but he knew that most crises in the office pass quickly and are of much less import than they appear at the time. Or as Yogi Berra might have put it: If you let it get to you, it will get you!

2. You should recognize that you may not understand the situation thoroughly. It may help to seek clarification for the reasons you did not get the raise or other benefit you expected. Perhaps there is some misunderstanding that, if corrected, would lead to a better outcome. You may acquire information that puts the problem in perspective. For example, your request for a new computer may have been turned down because there were too many requests to accommodate. Perhaps the situation will improve next year.

3. Although you were "nickel and dimed" this time, you may find that, on balance, more coins fall into your lap over time than you probably deserve.

4. Even if you are right about having been wronged, you never want to take actions that foreclose options in the future. Time has a way of healing most wounds. You may find that you are better off living to fight another day. If you stomp out and leave the firm over one incident, you will not be taking affirmative action to better your life. You will be letting your adversary dictate your course of action. Bide your time.

5. If you react too quickly, you may miss an opportunity to gain experience and judgment from the situation. You may profit from learning how you came up on the losing end of the issue.

6. No organization is perfect, particularly when it comes to compensation. If the organization is right about 80 percent of

the time, it is doing well by human standards. So for example, if your salary is within 10 percent of what it should be, you are doing well in any organization.

In dealing with organizational authority, you should be aware of the tendency to reenact your own early struggles with parents and teachers. Keep your perspective. Remember that the firm's partners are not a part of your personal history. Your senior partner is not the teacher who gave you an unfair grade or the parent who was (and perhaps still is) trying to control your life. It is always worth taking time to step back and see if you can take some of the stress and humiliation out of the equation. Reasonable people can differ on important issues.

Never act uncivilly. It will do nothing to enhance your career. Do not get involved in negative, backstabbing conversations. They lead to nothing productive. And if you have to change firms, do it without a fuss and put a good face on it afterward.

MENTORS

Mentors are important as your teachers and advocates. If your firm has a formal mentoring system, you will have an easy time finding a mentor with whom to start. However, most firms have relatively little in the way of formal mentoring, and where it does exist, it is often inadequate. As you proceed in your career in the firm, I recommend that you find an informal mentor or mentors by trying to work with a variety of lawyers whose professionalism you can emulate.

Finding a good mentor is a challenge. It is fair to assume that most of the lawyers in the firm will be happy to spend at least a few minutes mentoring you, particularly if you keep your request for guidance informal. However, it is important to learn who is most successful in the firm and seek those persons out. Choose wisely because success and failure are, unfortunately, contagious. Find a mentor or mentors who are reasonably pleasant and can offer constructive criticism without being overly critical.

Successful lawyers may be successful in different roles. In every firm there are "miners," "binders," and "grinders." The miners bring in business. The binders are those rare individuals who bring everyone together to work as a team (or at least avoid killing each other). The grinders perform the work that others bring in. As a new lawyer, you will be working as a grinder and will need to obtain input from successful grinders. You should, over time, befriend and observe miners and binders to learn their important skills. The best lawyers combine all of these roles.

Beware of misperceptions among associates concerning the relative success of lawyers in the firm. Associates frequently gravitate to easygoing partners who do not challenge them or to extroverted partners who readily befriend associates. Such partners may or may not teach well and may or may not have good skills to teach.

Older lawyers—often name partners—enjoy the company of younger lawyers. So make an effort to at least meet the people at the top of your organization. You would be surprised how much you will learn, not only about practicing law, but also about how to grow your business. The entrepreneurial veterans are usually the mainstay of a law firm. You will want to begin to acquire those skills, even if they do not appear to be readily applicable to your circumstances. Try to learn about their careers and techniques and to diplomatically pin them down on how they got to where they are. How did they market themselves? What skills did they develop? What types of connections were most helpful?

Finding a good mentor is always a challenge. Indeed, in a large firm, where misinformed associate gossip usually abounds, it is very difficult. Here are eight tips that will help.

1. See which lawyers are consistently sought after in the organization for their expertise and hard work. Almost by definition, these lawyers have more experience. After all, they have probably put in more hours than the other lawyers in the firm.

2. Try to find out which partners have the most financial clout in the organization. At the very least, these people know how to market the firm. It is often difficult to obtain this information accurately. Indeed, it has been my experience that in some firms this information is not really available even to the members of the firm. Often client originations are clouded by arbitrary formulas embedded in computers that allocate clients to the lawyers who originally brought them in, rather than to those in the firm to whom the clients now look for service. But you can see who is really handling which clients and make a judgment.

3. Ask the managing partner for some ideas if you feel it is appropriate. The managing partner is generally not interested in the job of mentor (and may not be suitable), but he or she will know all of the lawyers' strengths and weaknesses quite well. For example, if you are interested in learning about marketing, you could ask the managing partner to suggest someone who is good at it.

4. Give any lawyer to whom you have been principally assigned to work the opportunity of being your mentor, for diplomatic reasons, but keep your eyes open for informal mentors who may be better teachers of different skills.

5. *Find positive people and avoid negative people.* There is nothing less conducive to success than hanging around with people who do nothing but complain about the firm and their supervisors. Such people are on a path of self-destruction and will not help you get ahead. *Find the people who are winners and study what*

they do that makes them good lawyers. Please bear in mind that it is often comforting to enjoy the solidarity of a group of complainers, but it does not motivate you to do well.

6. Avoid "victims." The lawyer who believes that he has lost a case because the judge was against him or that he had a bad jury has missed the point. Assume that a good lawyer can win every case. Proactively seek out the good lawyers and learn to become one of them.

7. Avoid anyone who has serious personal problems. If you learn that a partner has been having affairs with associates, you can be sure that this is not a mentor you need. If the partner is a heavy drinker, he or she probably won't have extra sober time for you.

8. Do not be deceived by appearances as you try to learn the "pecking order" of the firm. As mentioned earlier, formal authority is frequently not the same as real authority in an organization. Indeed, the most powerful members of the firm may prefer to occupy no formal position. It may reflect the accurate perception that day-to-day administrative duties sap the energy of even the most dedicated attorneys.

When you find a mentor, you want to ask questions and obtain assignments from the mentor. Ask your mentor to help you evaluate your professional goals in the firm (not your ultimate desire to run for president of the United States or to start your own firm). Don't be afraid to ask for feedback from those for whom you work, but not too often. Excessive feedback may erode your confidence and tends to cause you to lose the forest for the trees.

By working hard for a good lawyer, you will immeasurably improve your opportunities for good assignments and good reviews. Hopefully your mentor will become your advocate and friend as well as your teacher. If you simply remain passive and rely on the firm to find someone to take you under his or her wing, you will neither enhance your career nor fully enjoy your experience in the firm.

WHAT PARTNERS TALK
ABOUT

If you are not paranoid, you can skip this section. If you are like the rest of us, at least to some degree, you may ask yourself what partners talk about besides politics and baseball.

Partners talk incessantly, very much the way associates do. But what they talk about is quite different, and it may differ depending on the firm. I am going to tell you what I have distilled from my years of listening to senior lawyers in different organizations in good times and bad.

1. Partners principally talk about their own compensation. Not surprisingly, this is the most intense conversation, and its consequences are far reaching. In positively charged firms, this can lead to an easing of tensions. In negatively charged firms, it can sometimes lead to a breakup of the firm.

2. Partners in positively oriented firms talk about getting business and hiring new lawyers. The focus is outward. They want to learn about opportunities for developing, or at least

improving, the firm. If this is not a major focus of the discussion, the organization is in trouble.

3. Partners talk about billings and collections. Money is a prime motivator of the partners in any enterprise and a law firm is no different.

4. Partners talk about each other, including a constant critique of the management. While some of this conversation is charitable conversation, I regret to say that in many cases, it is negative gossip.

5. Partners talk about committee concerns. This is a management function and is usually boring, but necessary.

6. Partners talk about associates. And contrary to what you probably believe, almost all of the conversation with respect to associates is positive. The owners of the firm have made a substantial economic and personal investment in the associates with whom they work. For the most part, their goal is for each associate to thrive in the organization and to either become a partner or leave for an even more rewarding career.

The bulk of the time spent on associates in partners' meetings is spent on allocation of scarce associate resources or the hiring of new associates. The rest of the time is spent on constructive ideas for improving the performance of the existing associates. This includes time spent on compensation of associates and the economics of associates (including billable hour requirements).

Some time is spent on associate reviews. However, this is generally seen as unpleasant work. While it may involve some negative comments, it is usually mixed in with some positive comments and efforts to be constructive. Ventilation about specific associates is, in my experience, rare, although over time good associates earn good reputations and poor associates earn guarded reputations.

Some time is spent on the selection of associates for partnership. This process in most firms is a positive one. The firm will either promote an associate or encourage the associate to find a new position where perhaps the relationship can continue. For proof of this, you have only to look at the large number of firms that promote associates to the rank of "counsel" or "non-equity" status. Most normal people don't like firing others, particularly younger colleagues whom they respect.

Overall, remarkably little time is spent on negative comment about associates or on gossip about them. There is no benefit to this type of conversation, and good lawyers don't want to spend too much time in useless meetings.

7.   Partners talk inordinately about intra-office sexual relationships, if there are any. Remember this when you contemplate what I said earlier about sexual etiquette.

What is striking about partner conversation is that it is important to associates, but they have no input. I do not think this is fair, but life is sometimes unfair. Since there is nothing you can do about it, just do the best work of which you are capable and let it go. In the end, worrying about that which you cannot influence is a bad habit—to which I have, unfortunately, been addicted myself. Now that I have warned you, you will at least have an opportunity to avoid this most malevolent addiction.

BECOMING A PARTNER

Partnership is seen as the "brass ring" of firm life, and the requirements for achieving it differ considerably from firm to firm. Some firms have a closed partnership, and it is difficult to become a member. Some make everyone a partner at a certain point in her or his career. Some require that you have developed your own business to become a partner. Some require that you be a hard worker. Some actually require that you be an outstanding lawyer.

Few new lawyers ever question whether partnership is a worthwhile goal. They assume it is, when it might not be. Here are some thoughts that will help you figure out whether the brass ring is worth it and how you can grab it successfully, if you think it is worth it.

Since becoming a partner is a business investment, you have to analyze the business benefits. It is true that in most firms partners make the best money, but it is not true that all partners make the best money.

Some firms pay junior partners poorly. Know whether yours is one of them. More importantly, you will want to know if your firm is "positioned" to grow and make money in its market. A first-class stateroom on the *Titanic* is not worth very much.

Some firms provide excellent training for associates but have limited partnership opportunities. You might choose to work for a few years in such a firm and then take a job in another firm or with a corporation where your future advancement is more certain. Or you might decide to move into a government agency to gain more experience and on-the-job training, with a view to returning one day to private practice.

If you decide to stay at a firm, it is obviously a good thing to become a partner and to become a member of the "inner sanctum" of the group. However, getting admitted requires planning. You have to find out how the group admits new members. What are the requirements?

In for-profit legal organizations, there are really only two questions presented for resolution in the partnership decision-making process:

1. Does the promotion of the candidate to partnership or leadership status add sufficient economic value to the organization to warrant a long-term commitment?

2. Can the firm afford to lose the candidate?

From these two questions arise the following subsidiary issues, which tend to consume the conversation:

1. Is there enough work in the candidate's area of expertise to warrant adding a partner?

2. Does the candidate control significant business?

3. Is the candidate a required "lieutenant" of a partner who controls significant business?

4. Is the candidate a competent lawyer (including lawyers with special expertise) who can add value by servicing existing clients?

5. Is the candidate economically productive? Can the candidate work hard and with independence on profitable business brought in by others?

6. Is the candidate "compatible" with the firm culture, including having the requisite interpersonal skills and ethical behavior?

When all is said and done, these are the fundamental calculations in almost all legal organizations. What differs between organizations in weighting these factors? Those firms with the view that the firm draws in the business, rather than the view that individual lawyers bring in the business, give great weight to competence in servicing clients and compatibility with the firm culture. The majority of the firms, however, consider control of business and economic productivity as more significant than interpersonal compatibility.

Obviously you cannot control the marketplace, which has been recently going through gyrations, and you cannot control the outcome of partnership decisions. However, if you want to be a partner, you should score well on all of these questions. At least you should be better than the average associate. Here are some tips I think can concretely improve your chances.

1. Follow any guidelines you are given. Many firms will give you general guidelines for becoming a member of the partnership. It is, of course, important to follow a path that achieves the stated requirements for promotion.

2. Make no enemies and try to please everyone. It may only take one partner at a meeting to nix your chances, particularly in small firms.

3. Think like an owner if you want to be an owner. You have to use good business judgment as well as good legal judgment. You have to act like you are willing to "own" the problems of the firm. For example, if there is too much work for you to handle, you should take responsibility for assisting your senior partner in finding someone to get it done.

4. Develop new business. It is always easier to get into the partnership if you control business.

5. Be certain, particularly in your fourth through eighth years, that you assume responsibility for cases and matters throughout their phases. Partners want to know that you can act responsibly on your own from soup to nuts.

6. Get to know all of the partners. The more people you know the better. The bigger the firm, the more difficult and essential this becomes. If you don't make an effort to meet people, they will not know you when your name comes up for partnership consideration.[57]

7. Build a close working relationship with one or more partners with business. A push from one of them will make a world of difference.

8. Obtain visibility in the community so that the firm can be proud of your achievements and knows that having made you a partner will be a feather in its cap.

I should add a word about governmental, nonprofit, and corporate promotion.

---

57. There is always debate about whether you are better off working for many lawyers or becoming an indispensable lieutenant of one. My short answer is that in the early years, it is generally good to work with a number of lawyers to advertise your skills and to learn more skills. In the later years, it makes sense to work with one or two senior lawyers who will be good mentors and advocates for your admission to the partnership.

The questions usually asked about whom to promote are similar to those asked in partnership meetings in for-profit legal organizations. There is, however, a different emphasis in the case of governmental and nonprofit organizations. These organizations are not concerned about your economic profitability, although your productivity is a significant factor. Teamwork, organizational skill, and compatibility are crucial, however. If you are abrasive, you become a problem for the organization. These organizations often put office politics ahead of competence in deciding whom to promote. Finally, they put emphasis on your ability to serve your captive clients. For example, if you are a federal prosecutor, it helps if the FBI and DEA write commendations of your work.

In in-house corporate law offices, economics play an important role, even if it is difficult to measure. Everyone in a corporation is required to show that they are "adding value" to the business. So if you have to give bad news to your business colleagues, be sure that you try to offer a lawful means for them to accomplish their business objectives. You want to be known as a lawyer who is sensitive to the interests of the company, as well as someone who can keep the company out of trouble. Politics plays a role in corporate promotion without doubt. So try to continually reach out to the business people in the company and keep up with the direction of the company and its financial objectives.

Finally, remember that partnership and promotion decisions are often unfair. You may have inadvertently offended someone. The business may be in an unexpected decline. Forces over which nobody has any control may have taken away your chance at the brass ring. Don't worry. This is not the end of the world. As much as you might want to, do not take it personally. There are plenty of brass rings out there; one of them is most certainly yours.

CHANGING FIRMS

I predict that you will one day switch jobs, even if you have made the perfect choice in the beginning and even if you become a partner. Most lawyers do. So here are some simple ideas that will improve the transition.

When switching jobs, it is not, as a general rule, advisable to tell your current employer that you are looking for a position.[58] This simply undermines your relationship and creates a needless disadvantage, since it may take some time to obtain a good position. Also be sure to obtain a strong commitment from the prospective employer before asking the current employer to serve as a reference.

---

58. There are certainly exceptions to this general rule. For example, a current employer might have good connections to help you land a job in a government agency or in a firm in another city. You have to assess the situation with some sensitivity, because once you announce that you are looking to leave, you are unlikely to be given lengthy or important assignments with your current firm.

Once you have decided to accept an offer with a new firm, always give the current firm sufficient notice to avoid a serious disruption to their work. Remember, as a lawyer, you have a paramount duty to your clients; leaving them in a situation in which they could be harmed is unacceptable.

It is always to your advantage to leave an employer on cordial terms. Your former employer will be a source of business and friendship. Whatever problems exist in your relationship today will almost always be forgotten in a few weeks if you handle the termination well. If you do not, the problems generated may perpetually, and unnecessarily, haunt you. As a lawyer, you may well inspire some people to dislike you no matter what you do. Avoid making former employers your enemies. Feelings of revenge have no place in the skill set of a successful lawyer because nobody ever really gets even. Success and success alone is the best revenge.

The mechanics of making a move are relatively straightforward. However, there are a number of practical questions that should be resolved before you make the move.

1. What will your salary be? Leaving a firm for small increments in salary is almost always a bad decision because the move will always involve a loss in your value. You will have to reestablish relationships with lawyers and clients. You will have no reservoir of goodwill based on your prior work and will have to "win your wings" all over again. Time and money are lost in this process. So be sure that there is a clearly offsetting gain—such as the opportunity to make a lot more money, to bring in more business, or to advance your skills dramatically.

2. Will you be given "credit" for the time you served in the first firm in terms of your seniority in the partnership track and your eligibility for benefits, such as pension plan participation? You may still decide to take the job even if the answers

are negative, but you cannot evaluate the opportunity if you do not know the answers.

3. What are the consequences for your insurance coverage? Be sure you understand the effect of a move on your medical coverage for preexisting illnesses. Double check to be certain that the new policy will cover such conditions immediately. Also think through your malpractice coverage. If you have been working for a firm, generally the old firm's insurance will cover you for past acts during your tenure there. If you have been carrying your own insurance, it may be necessary to purchase "tail" coverage, which can be quite expensive. Watch out for life insurance as well. Most firms provide life insurance coverage of some sort. Find out how much is available in the new firm. If you are losing coverage, you may wish to replace it while you are young and healthy.

4. What are the ramifications for your investments? If you have vested money in a 401(k) or other pension plan, remember to check on the time limits for moving it into a rollover IRA, in the event you choose to do so. The rules are complicated, and you should check with a tax advisor to ensure that you have no difficulty.

A word is in order about headhunters, the brokers who look to match lawyers with job openings. When you have a job you like, their constant pestering seems like a nuisance. When you don't have a job, or need to leave your current job, they may be a salvation. What you probably don't know is that they charge an arm and a leg. Indeed, their fees can be up to one-half of a year's salary. So consult with your network to see who is a good headhunter. And be sure, when you sign an agreement with them, to exclude those firms where you have personal contacts already. Your appeal to a new firm will be much greater if you can come "free of freight charges."

BEING FIRED: OPENING THE GOLDEN PARACHUTE

This is a portion of the book that I would rather not have to write. Unfortunately, from time to time in the real world, people are fired. For some, this is a traumatic event that has lasting negative consequences on their careers and lives. For others, it is a forced opportunity to develop and improve their careers. Understanding how to turn lemons into lemonade is critical. Believe me, however painful the moment, you will look back on it with humor at some point in the future. That point can be today.

Why are people fired? The ever-growing list of law firms laying off associates is sad testimony to the fact that firing is commonplace. Most lawyers are not fired for dishonesty or sloth. Most are fired for economic reasons over which they have never had any control.[59] Some are fired because they have not been productive in the environment of the firm in which they have been working because they have been assigned the wrong type of work. Some have been assigned to a partner who had unrealistic expectations or imperfect mentoring skills. And some are fired because of personal animosities or misconduct in which they have been involved. Understanding why you have been fired is the starting point for dealing with the situation constructively.

Personalizing your situation is always self-destructive. You were not fired because you were a bad person. You were not fired because you have no talent. You were not fired because people had it in for you. Whatever infinitesimal grain of truth there is in these bitter thoughts, they cannot be the reason you were fired because they make no economic sense, and firms are, in the end, economically driven institutions. If you had brought in $2 million in business, you probably would not have been fired, even if others thought you needed to develop your skills or polish your personality.

If you personalize the situation, you will be paralyzed. There is nothing you can do in the next three months to acquire the talent that you incorrectly think you don't have. You will not be able to become a "better person." You cannot undo the "conspiracy" against you. What you can do is to take charge, correctly analyze the circumstances leading up to your termination, and position yourself to get a better job. Over and over again, I have seen people who were "fired" turn their careers into monumental achievements. All of them had two things in

---

59. This phenomenon is particularly true as I write. Legions of lawyers are being laid off by some of the most prestigious firms because these firms simply could not weather the economic downturn without dramatic cost reduction.

common: they did not hold grudges against their former employers, and they learned from their mistakes.

So step one is to figure out why you were fired. As we discussed earlier in the book, new associates are generally not economically profitable for reasons over which they have no control. They are generally costly and almost always inefficient. If your firm is in a general economic downturn, or if the owners think they are involved an economic downturn, you may be cut, even though it is unfair. Nonetheless, the owners may make it seem like they are dissatisfied with your work. The reason for any purported dissatisfaction may simply arise from the fact that it is hard for entrepreneurs to tell you they have failed, either in generating new business or in mentoring new associates. Usually, no associate is a "failure" in the workplace. It is simply a question of efficiency: how long it takes him or her to get the job done right. If the efficiency is too low for the type of work on hand, the profitability of the associate falls.

Some associates do get into interpersonal trouble within the firm. This usually involves abrasive encounters with partners, some of whom are also insecure. Rather than backing down and politely diffusing the situation, the associate engages in unproductive bickering—either directly with the partner or indirectly with other associates (remember that everything you say gets back to the partners). Either way, the associate becomes an additional drain on the organization and goes on the chopping block. Here it is wise to remember the biblical proverb that "he who troubleth his own house shall inherit the wind."[60]

There are reasons why associates "act out." It almost always involves a test of authority, an unwillingness to accept constructive criticism from partners, "class warfare" over

---

60. *Proverbs* 11:29.

compensation, or hasty judgments about partners and the firm. Because new associates have never been owners, they typically don't think like owners and don't act like owners. Thankfully, the mistakes are not incurable if you understand what has happened and take concrete steps to avoid abrasive situations in the future. If you become the diplomat you never were, you will thrive. But if you continue these habits in a new job, you will repeat the situation over and over until it defeats you.

Finally, there are associates whose work habits are seriously defective (e.g., they don't turn in timesheets) or their judgment is very poor (e.g., they engage in sexual harassment of secretaries). They don't work well because they seemingly can't work well. If you are in this group, don't give up hope. Remember, you made it through law school, which means that you have the basic judgment and skill necessary to be a lawyer. I have two suggestions, both of which can be valuable to all lawyers. First, get professional help, using the resources of your firm's health insurance. An objective and trained observer can help you see and resolve the dysfunction. Second, if judgment is not your strongest suit, find somebody whose judgment is impeccable to use as a sounding board. The wisest people are usually those who listen carefully to what others with better judgment have to say.

Happily, most terminations are not life threatening as long as you remember two things: First, firing is impersonal not personal. You are still a good person and have potential that can be realized in a different environment. The lucky thing is that you found your incompatibility with your firm earlier rather than later. Second, you have an opportunity to find another job that will improve your life. As Winston Churchill once quipped: "Success is moving from one failure to another without losing your enthusiasm!"

Here are some good ideas for dealing with termination:

1. Try to leave your firm on the best possible terms. Ideally you will negotiate a robust "severance package," which gives you the opportunity to find a job. If this is not possible, ask for some money to compensate you for the job-search period. Remember, depending on the size of the firm, you generally have a right to continue your health insurance at your expense for eighteen months (COBRA). Don't let it lapse![61]

2. Try to negotiate a recommendation. Most firms will at least be neutral in what they tell prospective employers. Usually one or more of the partners will be happy to give you a good recommendation.

3. Ask the firm for help in outplacement. One or more of the partners may be able to place you. Also ask if they can they recommend a good headhunter.

4. Ask if the firm will let you keep working (or at least stay on the payroll) until you find a job.[62] At least they should let you keep your voice mail and e-mail so that it appears you are still employed.

5. Ask if the firm will pay for mental health counseling for you to get through the stress of the termination. You would be surprised at how many firms would be willing to do this, particularly since their insurance plan will already pick up part of the tab.

Now that you know you will be leaving, you must do what you can to ensure you will have the resources to be careful and patient in making your next job selection. Get advice from

---

61. If you are in good health, you may be able to obtain less costly private insurance.

62. Interestingly, some firms have agreed to pay laid-off associates who work in legal aid the going rate for legal-aid lawyers for one year.

good headhunters to avoid repeating the same problems. Then look for a job where economic factors don't undermine your productivity. If a firm has a lot of small cases for small clients, your inefficiency will be a clear detriment unless you improve quickly (which can be done). If the cases are big and the clients are wealthy, you will have opportunities to build your efficiency without costly write-offs.

Once you are free of the firm, there are several important steps you must follow to maximize your potential.

1. Do not rule out possible jobs too quickly. Usually you won't initially have enough information to make a good final decision about what you are ultimately going to do in your career. Everything should be on the table. Brainstorm with your friends, headhunters, and former professors. The fascinating thing about the law is the fact that you can always "reinvent" yourself. You can become an expert on almost anything.

2. Apply for as many jobs as you can. By ruling out the firm you are leaving, you have made the task of getting a job a little easier, but it is still a statistical game. If you can, keep an open mind about changing geographical location.

3. Contact your law school placement office for advice.

4. Prepare a good resume.

5. Never speak ill of your former employer. Remember, firms look for team players. It you are too sharp a critic of your former employers, you will not impress new employers. It tends to make new employers nervous that there was some personal animosity at the old firm, which may be imported into the new firm. Since the odds are overwhelmingly high that you were not fired for personal reasons, why make it look that way?

6. Pay particular attention to ethical rules concerning conflicts with new firms and old clients.

7. Don't steal files. And be sure that you do not solicit your old firm's clients until after you have left.

8. Try to cultivate your old enemies. All the irritation of your former situation will be erased in a few weeks, and you will become a distinguished alumnus of your former firm.

9. Keep hope alive. Don't panic. Everything will work out. You got a job before and you will get one again. I don't care how bad the market looks; you *will* get a job.

Interviewing with new firms presents some challenges. It is wise to be honest about your reasons for leaving without dwelling on them too much. Many firms will understand that the environment of the firm you have left is one that was not a good measure of your potential. Keep the focus of your interviews forward looking. You can improve your chances with your boundless enthusiasm.

Finally, it is worth paying some heed to the words of President Bill Clinton, who addressed the following to his daughter's high school graduation class:

> I urge you not to succumb to hatred or self-pity. We all give in to them now and then, of course, but you need to work at snapping out of it and going on. Hatred and self-pity give victory to the very dark forces we deplore. Despair guarantees defeat. Cynicism is a cowardly cop-out. And no one ever really gets even in life.[63]

---

63. THE WASHINGTON POST, June 7, 1997.

WOMEN IN
THE LAW FIRM

If you are a man, don't stop reading. The role of women in the law firm is just as critical to men as it is to women. It impacts on the structure of law firms, their economics, and ultimately the profitability and quality of their work product. Moreover, in the twenty-first century, when men are taking a much more active role in parenting, much of this chapter is of immediate practical significance to you.

The role of women in law firms has changed radically in the past fifty years. After she had completed a brilliant three years at a major law school in the early 1950s and a clerkship on the Second Circuit, the mother of one of my friends was told directly by the leading Wall Street firms that she need not apply because they never hired women. Indeed, women were not found in significant numbers in law schools until the 1970s. Today the situation has changed substantially due to economic demands, which usually require two spouses to work, and legal regulation of the workplace, which prohibits gender discrimination.

The fact remains, however, that women are dramatically underrepresented in the higher echelons of most large law firms. In 2007, NALP found that women constituted 45.06 percent of associates, but only 18.34 percent of partners.[64] Unfortunately, this situation is unlikely to change quickly for two reasons.

First, many men still undermine women in the workplace in ways that are subtle, pernicious, and counterproductive. Rather than promoting women as leaders in their firms, some firms regrettably prefer to promote men. Even in meetings I have noticed an unwillingness by some men to give leading roles to women, based upon a notion that clients see men as better "authority figures." Second, women tend to drop out of the partnership competition to raise children, slowing their statistical rate of progression.

---

64. NALP, *Minority Women Still Underrepresented in Law Firm Partnership Ranks—Change in Diversity of Law Firm Leadership Very Slow Overall* (NALP 2007), available at http://www.nalp.org, last visited September 9, 2009. The not-for-profit organization Catalyst, which works to promote women in business, has estimated that at current rates of growth, women will not achieve parity with men in the partnership ranks until the year 2086. Catalyst, *Women in Law in the U.S.* (May 2009), available at http://www.catalyst.org, last visited September 9, 2009. A very recent survey by The National Association of Women Lawyers has recently shown that 72% of large law firms have no women among the top five rainmakers and 46% have *no* women in their top ten rainmakers. The National Association of Women Lawyers, *Report of the Fourth Annual National Survey on Retention and Promotion of Women in Law Firms, October 2009*, available at http://nawl.org, last visited January 12, 2010.

While many of the overt acts of gender bias that character-ized earlier times have been deterred, there is a lot of subtle stereotyping of women and their place in law firms and other legal organizations. To give but a few examples, women are sometimes seen as more "compassionate," better "binders," and less productive "second-income spouses."[65] At best, these are interesting and unproved sociological hypotheses; at worst, they are prejudiced, sexist views.

Whatever sociologists may ultimately find about women, and whatever the statistical norms may ultimately turn out to be,[66] stereotypes are unacceptable guides for operating individual organizations, where particular women have unique profiles. I believe that women can be as productive and inspired in the prac-tice of law as men because I have seen it throughout my career. Like other lawyers, they have to act with confidence, set goals, and keep a focused determination to succeed in the practice.

It is difficult to deal with a firm that consistently under-mines women in a significant way, except to advise you that it is rarely in the interest of a woman to stay in such a firm. Some women in chauvinist firms do make money on what might be loosely called "tokenism." But it is generally wise to remember the old adage that the "medium is the message." You need a

65. One of the most bizarre manifestations of recent gender stereotyping occurred when Freshfields Bruckhaus Deringer, an international firm based in the U.K., suggested that its women lawyers wear high heels and skirts to "embrace their femininity." The Wall Street Journal Law Blog, last visited December 28, 2008.

66. An interesting exploration of some of the sociological and psychologi-cal literature is found in Linda Babcock and Sara Laschever, WOMEN DON'T ASK—NEGOTIATION AND THE GENDER DIVIDE (Princeton University Press, 2003). The book argues that women are often afraid to negotiate salaries and working conditions. While this is not a full explanation of the gender gap in law, it is well worth keeping in mind from the very outset of your career.

supportive atmosphere in which to flourish. If the air is bad, you have to move.

You can, of course, stay and change things by persistent advocacy and occasional confrontation, but I do not advocate this approach. It wastes too much time for too little benefit in most cases. Ultimately the really chauvinist firms tend to have other irrationalities that make them poor places to work.

Nor do I subscribe to the view that women can overcompensate for bias by "being more aggressive," "being more assertive," or "being themselves." It is the nature of stereotyping that whatever you do, an equal and opposite stereotype emerges (e.g., "Gee, she is a b——.", "She is pushy."). If you find yourself in an organization where you are impeded significantly by stereotyping, move on. Likewise avoid firms that have very few women. The role of a pioneer is not, as I noted earlier, to be envied.

If you are in an organization that basically supports women, you can overcome the "residual" bias that may lurk by doing what everyone has to do. *Be confident; you are qualified. Improve your core competence and service to clients. Ask for better assignments. Market yourself and your firm endlessly.* Build your economic strength. Be assertive in the normal way that lawyers should be in representing clients. And whatever you do, avoid subconsciously buying into the stereotypes about women. Poor as the overall statistics may be, there are plenty of women who are leaders in the profession and top rainmakers in firms in this country. In a changing world, you can be one of them.

It is worth repeating that if you are unhappy with your job, ask for better work or conditions. The people for whom you work are not your enemies. As a general rule, they want you to be happy. But they cannot read your mind and are often unaware of inequities, even obvious inequities. Your environment is not fixed; you can influence it.

Chances are that you will not avoid all bias in your life. Set limits on bias where you see it; but if the bias is inadvertent, set the limits in a way that reaffirms the worth of the offender and of the firm. And, of course, if you are subjected to harassment, report it immediately to your organization's management. All successful organizations want to have the information immediately so that they can take prompt ameliorative actions.

A second and equally significant issue for women in the law is the "drop-out factor." Women tend to drop out to raise children and run the home. These are worthy objectives; however, it is often quite costly to the women and to their organizations. Women lawyers have spent as much time on the development of their legal skills as men. They have spent an enormous amount of money on their education. Simply dropping out is a huge loss, which probably cannot be recouped in later years if the women return to work. From the firm's point of view, each lawyer is an enormous investment, and a lawyer who becomes unproductive or who leaves the firm is a great loss.

So how can all of this be reconciled? I have no quick panacea to offer. But my belief is that if the parties are properly motivated and understand the true economics, this can be a win-win situation. Here is how.

The principal stress for women in law firms is the competing demands of clients and family. Modification of familial demands is possible only to an extent. Nannies, housekeepers, and husbands can all help, but they cannot, and should not, provide all that is required. There are 168 hours in a week. A firm can demand up to sixty. Commuting demands another five. Sleep can demand fifty-six. This leaves forty-seven hours for family life and basic functions. That is very little.

Not all women are superwomen, but everyone can become better organized. Fifty well-organized and focused hours in the firm are worth more than seventy-five poorly organized hours. So always begin with organization and time management.

Next, confront the issue of productivity in the workplace in a constructive manner. If necessary, you should ask your firm if it would agree to "flex time" or "deferred partnership track" or even "job sharing." Although the traditional wisdom is that law is such a demanding profession that only full-time commitment can succeed, I think the truth is that there are many ways in which lawyers can work part time, as long as their economic demands are in line with their productivity. If everyone keeps an open mind, everyone can win. There are certainly times when full-time attention to work is required (e.g., trying a case or preparing to try one). But most of the time, there is a great deal of flexibility, and you can even work at home.[67]

Many women, of course, prefer to work full time and find that by structuring their hours to provide quality time to their families, they can get along quite well. I came from a family where my mother and other women worked full time. I can assure you that I survived perfectly well. Today, in an age where communication with children while at work is so greatly enhanced by technology and where fathers are rightly expected to be more involved in their children's lives, no child should feel abandoned by parents who have to work.

---

67. There is empirical evidence which strongly supports the view that part-time partners can be very successful in their firms. For a detailed analysis and some ideas for handling the process, *see,* Cynthia Thomas Calvert, *Reduced Hours, Full Success: Part-Time Partners in U.S. Law Firms,* (The Project for Attorney Retention September 2009) available at http://nawl.org, last visited January 12, 2010.

Another possible solution for women who have difficulty juggling family and work responsibilities is to find positions in corporations and government where working hours can be better structured and limited. This career choice enables many women to organize their lives better. The difficulty is that corporations and government are still clients that make huge demands. For the highly motivated individual, the time spent may be just the same as that spent in a firm. And the stress of most of these jobs is still very great. In fact, when I look back on my own career, I tend to believe that my years as a government prosecutor were far more stressful than my years in law firms.

Finally, you should never lose sight of the fact that legal organizations need women very much. There will always be competition for quality lawyers. Arbitrarily limiting the employment pool is foolish for any firm. Furthermore, there is a large network of women in law across the country who want to send work to other women. This network, if properly engaged, can produce a great deal of work for firms. And many firms rightly believe that pushing minorities and women forward is a strong policy simply because it is the right thing to do. As lawyers, we are bound to uphold the law and to promote justice. If we take any pride in our profession, we should take pride in promoting its diversity and its openness to new groups. Many of us came from groups that the profession traditionally shunned. So we all have a stake in the success of women and minorities. We all need to keep pushing.

MINORITIES IN
THE LAW FIRM

The challenges presented to minority lawyers in the law are substantial, despite the genuine efforts of most legal organizations to recruit and promote minorities. My own law firm has received considerable recognition for its work in this area, but I think that there remains a lot to do to improve the opportunities for minority lawyers throughout the profession. As a new lawyer, it makes very little difference that the organization for which you work has made great strides. It has to impact you in a personal and meaningful way. It is not a statistical game; it is a personal challenge.[68]

---

68.   In speaking of minorities, I include gay and lesbian lawyers as well. The organizations for which I have worked have all tried to fully accept lawyers without regard to sexual orientation. And I like to think that the legal profession has been more enlightened than others in this area. However, there is a significant lack of statistical data on the success of GLBT lawyers in the profession (*see*, NALP, *Law Firms Report More GLBT Lawyers, But Numbers Remain Small*, NALP BULLETIN, November 2008, available at http:// www.nalp.org, last visited September 1, 2009). This can be attributed not only to sensitivity about collecting the information, but also to a continued

The statistics are grim enough. Minority lawyers are often heavily recruited by law firms, but rarely become partners. For example, according to NALP, in 2008, 19.08 percent of associates were minorities, but only 5.92 percent of partners were minorities.[69] The attrition rate is astounding.

While many women drop out of law firms for lifestyle reasons, for the most part minorities leave because they become disenchanted with the firm. The reason that has been given for the great attrition of minorities is that affirmative action recruiting brings in candidates with lower law school grades.[70] The new associates are less productive, and the firm gives them the message that they should leave. I believe, however, that the truth is much more complicated.

There is very little empirical study that directly links law school grades to lawyer performance. Intuitively, one would think that there must be some correlation. After all, diligent students must be diligent lawyers. But the truth is that for anyone to graduate from law school and pass the bar examination requires higher than average intelligence. Moreover, even

---

phobia about the issue. In the absence of such reporting, one should assume that some law firms are discriminating against GLBT lawyers in much the same way the society as a whole does. Moreover, most organizations continue the society's practice of discrimination with respect to employment benefits with regard to domestic partners. If you are in the GLBT group, my advice is to network extensively to learn more about firms' practices. NALP has substantial resources available online at http://www.nalp.org to assist you in locating organizations to contact. NALP also asks law firms in its questionnaire about openly gay lawyers in their firms, but the reported data is so insignificant that the responses are really not that helpful.

69. *See, Women and Minorities in Law Firms by Race and Ethnicity*, NALP BULLETIN, available at http://www.nalp.org, last visited September 14, 2009.

70. Sander, *supra* note 5.

the most cynical observer would have to concede that law firms would not engage such economically self-destructive behavior as to hire 19 percent of their associates with the understanding that most were incompetent. So it is preposterous to say that minority lawyers cannot be good lawyers. The logic is flawed, and such thinking is not at all helpful to the individual lawyer or legal organization.[71]

What happens to minority lawyers? When they arrive, they are generally as eager as any new lawyers. However, the dynamic that ensues is not always favorable. There is empirical evidence that minority lawyers do not receive the mentoring or the assignments they need to succeed.[72] Undoubtedly there is some stereotyping that occurs. It is possible that partners may be more sensitive to errors made by minority associates than other associates; however, on the other side of the coin, minority lawyers may be a bit more sensitive to criticism. There is a natural insecurity in believing that you were hired based upon some criterion other than your "legal ability." Often there is some isolation simply because of a minority status. All this interferes with the smooth interpersonal relations, which must be the basis of a good working environment.

What does this mean for you if you are a minority yourself? The answer is: very little if you want to succeed. As a minority lawyer, you can succeed in most legal organizations if you apply yourself to it. Ignore the statistics. They do not control your life or your destiny. They are the results from the study of other people and other law firms. Your organization wants and needs you.

---

71. James E. Coleman and Mitu Gulati, *Response to Professor Sander: Is It Really About Grades?*, 84 N.C. LAW REV. 1823 (2006).
72. *Id.*

So get a mentor, work hard, and look for good assignments. Solicit criticism of your work in detail so that you can improve and get the most out of your experience. Network, market, and improve your skills inside and outside of the firm, using the techniques that are set out in this book. Know that there is no economic benefit to a firm for you to fail. On the contrary, the firm needs you to succeed. There is no reason for you to be an historical statistic.

Focus on Gandhi's famous observation that we have to be the change we want to see in the world. *If you feel that you are not getting good assignments, go to the lawyers working on good cases and ask for better work.* If you need more mentoring, go out and get yourself another mentor. The worst that can happen is that some partners will ignore you, but the odds are good that your initiative will be taken in a positive way. Remember that initiative and team play tend to trump everything else in any organization. As I said earlier with respect to women in the law firm, you have to ask for what you want and need. *Be confident. The worst thing you can do is to endure pain without speaking up or quit when you have a good possibility of improving your conditions.*

Do not be embarrassed that you may have been hired, in part, for your minority status. Plenty of lawyers have been hired for reasons other than their success in taking tests in law school. Many have been hired because they were well connected, their parents were clients, and their "pedigree" was impeccable. Your success will be no less deserved than theirs. After a short time in a legal organization, it will not matter how you got there. All that will matter is what you can do in the firm.

The legal profession was traditionally very prejudiced. Irish Americans, Jews, women, gays, and African Americans were all kept out of good firms deliberately. But as I have said, in my lifetime things have changed a great deal. Firms now realize the necessity of diversity, even if they do not fully embrace or understand its true advantages. The door is open. Now is the time to walk in and achieve. Remember that good lawyering is learned behavior. You are qualified!

ACHIEVING FINANCIAL INDEPENDENCE

Personal financial management should be an integral part of your strategic plan as a new lawyer. Lawyers who cannot manage their own money cannot manage the many complex issues presented by their clients. Whether you are in a high-paying commercial firm or a low-paying public interest firm, your financial discipline at home and at work will enhance your professional achievements. In the worst case, bankruptcy can ruin a lawyer's reputation. In the best case, proper management can insulate you from many of the personal crises the profession can visit upon you from time to time.

Given the current economic situation, it may be hard to consider saving and investing the money you make as a lawyer. The temptation is to believe that it is irrelevant in the midst of chaos. I assure you, however, that it is more relevant than ever and that personal finances need to take a prominent place in the life of every lawyer—especially new lawyers. The knowledge you acquire now and the disciplines you adopt will make all the difference in your life.

Over the years, I have been asked countless times by new lawyers and others to help them get started saving for their future. I began investing in the stock market over forty-five years ago, at the age of sixteen, and have spent a lifetime studying personal finance, starting with rather careful instruction by a financial planner who had himself weathered the crash of 1929. In the course of this effort, I have found some reliable ways for you to plan and achieve financial independence, which are, frankly, at some variance with the "conventional wisdom." That wisdom, of course, is that you should put all of your money in stocks, because that is where the highest returns are available over time. Even now, after so much financial turmoil, this continues to be the prevailing view. I still hear commentators arguing that over any twenty-year period in history, stocks are the leading performers.[73]

As I write, people around the world are tensely watching the stock markets after having seen much of their wealth evaporate. Believe me, I am a calm investor with a good deal of experience, but I am not immune to this tension. Unfortunately, this volatility and uncertainty is likely to continue for some time. And yet, *there is no alternative to investing.* As you earn, you have to save for retirement, and investment is part of that program. The key has been, and always will be, to control your risk.

Of course, you may still want to do as I have done and secure the advice of competent professionals. But you must

---

73.   *But see,* Sam Mamudi, *Rethinking Stocks' Starring Role,* THE WALL STREET JOURNAL, September 2, 2009 (reporting on some financial professionals now challenging the prevailing view that stocks should be a dominant investment for individuals).

be aware that these professionals have their own financial goals that are often incongruent with yours. Given the lackluster (or worse) performance of the so-called experts in this economic downturn (and even before that), you have to treat their advice with appropriate skepticism—which means *a lot* of skepticism. The stark reality is that as unpleasant as it may be, you are solely responsible for saving and investing your money. The odds are overwhelming that nobody can do it better than you.

What I have said about investment consultants also applies to mutual funds. Such funds are run by professionals who take a substantial fee for their advice. Over 90 percent of these professionals do not beat the market; as an individual investor, you will never find the 10 percent who do. Consider the fact that many college endowments and pension funds turned their money over to Bernard Madoff on his promise of substantially better than average returns, only to find that he stole their money. If major institutions cannot find good fund managers, you never will. Nor is there any reason to believe that your local broker has any greater wisdom in choosing managers.

If you have no experience with financial planning, you should begin by learning about different investments. I recommend that you begin by reading one of the basic primers on personal financial planning, which are widely sold in bookstores.[74] Learn a bit about the jargon and the basic concepts. Then you are ready to begin.

---

74. For example, I recommend Suze Orman's books THE ROAD TO WEALTH: THE MONEY BOOK FOR THE YOUNG, FABULOUS AND BROKE (Riverhead Books, 2005); WOMEN & MONEY: OWNING THE POWER TO CONTROL YOUR DESTINY (Spiegel & Grau, 2007); and SUZE ORMAN'S 2009 ACTION PLAN (Spiegel & Grau, 2009).

The first thing to know about investing is the importance of preserving your capital. All too often, mutual funds and brokers try to tout the enormous returns they have achieved for their clients over the past two years, three years, or five years. What they never tell you is the amount of risk they took to achieve these results. Since you are working hard for your money, you don't want to lose it. If you begin early, you can make money by patiently investing in safer investments.

Safety in investing is principally of two types: (1) safety from losing the investment because the issuer of the security falls on hard times, and (2) safety from economic trends, including falling demand, interest rate fluctuation, and inflation. For example, buying a thirty-year bond issued by the U.S. Treasury gives you the safety of your principal and interest payments, but it puts you at the mercy of inflation for thirty years. If the interest rate paid on your bond falls below the inflation rate, the "real interest" rate becomes negative and the value of the bond falls. Apart from inflation, if interest rates generally increase, the lower rate of interest paid on your bond will decrease its value. Thus, thirty-year U.S. Treasury bonds are considered high-risk investments because they are long-term investments, the value of which fluctuates dramatically with changes in inflation data and interest rates. By contrast, the stocks of major "blue chip" companies will generally grow in value to counteract inflation, but often do not pay much of a dividend and have a risk of financial downturn depending on the fortunes of the economy and the company.

It's often said that when you are young, you can take more risk. This is true, but only to a degree. Few people will make money for long by taking exceptional risks. Consider how well you will do at a roulette wheel, even if your "time horizon" is relatively long. Moreover, young and inexperienced investors are inherently more likely to make mistakes, which only compound the problem. Here youth does not always work in your favor.

The best method I know to control risk is to invest in "blue chip" investments, whether bonds or stocks, and to diversify the investments. With quality investing you can use your youth to hold the investments over a substantial period and make money. Investment advisors rarely stress this because they usually make their money on the basis of the number of trades you make. Therefore the strategy of buying securities and holding them for long periods of time cuts their remuneration over the short term. Rest assured this is the only way they are likely to look at it.

It is important to remember and to use the power of compounding. This is the enormous growth in your investment when you constantly reinvest the interest or dividends. For example, if you simply put $2,000 per year into a CD in an IRA for thirty years at just 5 percent, you will have $132,878 for retirement.

SAVING CASH

Every young lawyer should start her or his "portfolio" by saving at least six to eight months of salary. This is protection against unemployment and unforeseen expenses. Having cash promotes your independence in an uncertain world and improves your self-confidence.

Saving, of course, is a discipline. Like all disciplines, it is learned behavior. If you lack the discipline, try creating and living by a budget and having savings deducted from your checking account automatically. You will generally find that you can save a lot of money without a dramatic change in lifestyle.

One excellent way of saving cash for emergencies is to set up an online account with an Internet bank such as http://www.ingdirect.com or http://www.hsbcdirect.com. These banks are FDIC insured, and they pay a higher rate of interest than you can usually get from the bank you use for checking. You can set up an automatic transfer every month from your checking account.

CERTIFICATES OF DEPOSIT

Depending upon rates, some of your cash reserve can be put into Certificates of Deposit. These are often overlooked vehicles for investment. CDs up to $250,000 are federally insured.[75] They involve *no risk* other than the risk of inflation. Presently there are banks offering CDs at rates up to 4.25 percent (depending on duration) compounded daily, monthly, or semiannually. This means that they can be used to get the most out of compounding. Additionally, CDs generally offer protection of your principal from market fluctuations. In an emergency, you can cash in your CD early and pay a penalty of three or six months of interest (look for the smallest penalty when you invest). Thus you do not suffer the risk of fluctuations in principal

---

75. The current $250,000 limit is only in force until December 31, 2013, and then it returns to $100,000. It is possible that the increased limit will be renewed, but if you want to be safe, never put more than $100,000 in any bank past 2013. Remember, too, that if you leave your interest in the CD to compound, you must be careful that the combined total amount of interest and principal does not exceed the FDIC limit.

that is involved with stocks or bonds.[76] You can find the best rates by looking online at http://www.bankrate.com or http://www.moneyaisle.com. Since deposits in banks are insured, you can send your money to any bank in the country, confident that you will get it back.

CLEANING THE SLATE: ERASE YOUR CREDIT CARD DEBT

Most new lawyers have debt. Most of it is school debt. It is beyond the scope of this book to tell you how to handle school debt, except to warn you against debt consolidators. They are parasites. Keep paying the minimum on your school loans as long as the rates are favorable.

After you have an emergency cash fund of six to eight months of living expenses, *you must, however, erase your credit card debt.* Apart from reducing your FICO score, that algorithm that determines the interest rate on your car loan and credit lines, a credit card is the single worst financial tool you can use. Unless you pay the entire balance every month, you will be charged such exorbitant rates that you will *never* be able to save any money. You will achieve grinding poverty and no financial independence. You are paying up to 32 percent interest on unpaid balances. Nobody can afford that. Cut up the cards and

---

76. The stability of principal is true of CDs purchased directly from banks. It is not true for "brokered CDs" purchased through a brokerage firm. Brokered CDs are only guaranteed to return your principal at maturity. In the interim they can be sold, but the amount you receive will depend on market conditions. Thus brokered CDs are only recommended for purchasers who can hold until maturity. The interest on brokered CDs is not compounded in the CD. It is periodically paid into your brokerage account, where you must reinvest it.

use debit cards unless you pay on time every month the entire amount due.[77]

ASSET ALLOCATION

Once you have saved six to eight months' salary and erased your credit card debt, you are ready to invest in something a little more daring. Here is my recommendation for an ultimate goal: Invest one-third of your money in cash and bonds, invest one-third in your house, and invest one-third in stock index funds. In the case of stocks, invest a certain steady amount each month or quarter rather than putting all your money into investments at once. This "dollar cost averaging" of your investments allows you to moderate the effects of market fluctuations. If the market goes down, you buy at lower prices. If the market goes up, the value of your previous purchases goes up.

Dollar cost averaging can be set up as an automatic function. For example, you can simply send money to Vanguard with instructions to dollar cost average a specified amount of the money every month into an index fund. The methods for setting up automatic dollar cost averaging are endless.

BONDS

I recommend that as you save money, you begin by buying some bonds. If you have less than $25,000 to invest, the only bonds that can be purchased without risk are savings bonds, treasury notes, and treasury bills. Savings bonds come in different types with different maturities, and they can be purchased

---

77. You should be aware that in the current economic environment, credit card companies may cut your credit limits back as you pay off the debt. Hopefully this will serve an ameliorative function in your life.

in small denominations.[78] Treasury bills are short-term debt of the U.S. Treasury, which is repaid within one year. Treasury notes are repaid in less than ten years. Given the likelihood of increased inflation, it is best to keep the investment short term so that it can be reinvested when rates climb. You can purchase the notes and bills without commission directly from the Treasury at http://www.treasurydirect.com.

There are also two other potential types of bonds commonly marketed to the beginning investor: Treasury Inflation-Protected Securities ("TIPS") and corporate "internotes." Both can be purchased in small denominations without commissions. TIPS are issued by the U.S. Treasury and give you a fixed rate of interest, but the principal value is adjusted up and down according to an inflation formula. These are complex instruments with tax complications. In my view, they are not worth what you pay for them. Internotes are bonds issued by corporations in small denominations. Here the problem is credit risk. While it is probable that GE will repay its notes maturing in two or three years, there is no guarantee of such repayment. If you are frightened, stay with CDs.

When you have saved $50,000 to $100,000, you are ready to invest in municipal bonds, one of my favorite investments. These are best purchased in blocks of $25,000 or more. These are bonds issued by municipalities around the country and have the advantage of paying interest that is not taxed by the IRS, and, if issued by your state, generally not taxed by it.[79] This

---

78.   Although such bonds currently pay low interest, they do have some tax advantages, including the fact that they and other U.S. Treasury paper are not subject to state and local taxation.

79.   There are a few states which tax the income from their own bonds. As with all tax matters, it is wise to consult a professional.

freedom from income tax, combined with limited risk, make municipal bonds a good value over the long haul. A municipal bond carrying a 5 percent "yield" pays a taxable equivalent yield of almost 8 percent with almost no risk if you are in the 35 percent tax bracket. Historically the stock market has only returned about 9 percent and involves a lot of risk and volatility.

The risks of municipal bonds are as follows: First, like any fixed-income security, there is a risk that interest rates will rise and that the interest rate you will receive will be less than the "market" rate. Second, there is a risk of inflation eating away at the value of the bonds. Third, the bonds may not be easy to sell before their maturity without a loss, depending on market conditions. Finally, there is a risk that the issuing municipality will default.[80]

Here's how to minimize these risks. Buy only bonds rated AA or better by Standard and Poor's and Moody's. Buy only general obligation bonds of a state or revenue bonds supported by very reliable revenues, such as water and sewer revenues. Stay away from other revenue bonds that constitute a lien only on revenues of a particular, perhaps small and uncertain, municipal project. Revenue bonds, other than those issued by water and sewer authorities, have too much risk right now for the novice investor.

Many bonds carry "insurance" from companies such as AMBAC, MBIA, FGIC, and FSA. The idea of the insurance is to enhance the underlying credit and ratings of municipal bonds by insuring the timely payment of interest and principal. Unfortunately many of the insurance companies are themselves

---

80. There is also thought to be a risk that Congress will at some future point, prior to maturity, decide to tax municipal interest. I consider this to be a remote risk at the present time.

nearly underwater. Thus the insurance should not be used to replace an analysis of the credit of the issuing municipality.

You should try to "ladder" your portfolio of bonds so that you have 10 percent of your bonds coming due in each year for the next ten years. As a bond falls due, reinvest it in a new ten-year bond. Laddering in this way helps minimize the risk of interest rate change because you always reinvest 10 percent of your money each year and obtain the benefit of better rates if rates go up. Likewise you still have 90 percent invested at the old rates if interest rates go down. Because you have avoided bonds that are issued for longer than ten years, you are better protected against drops in the principal value of the bonds should you need to sell them prior to maturity. Remember, longer maturity bonds tend to be more volatile in the market if you try to sell prior to maturity.

In selecting municipal bonds, you need to know a few more parameters. First, you do not want bonds that are subject to the alternative minimum tax ("AMT"). Brokers understand the importance of avoiding AMT, but you should raise the issue. Second, many bonds have features in which the issuer can redeem the bond prior to maturity. These "call" features can seriously affect your ladder as well as your yield. Find out about the calls, and make sure that you have some assurance that the bond will be around to pay you interest for a substantial period of time. Also ask what the "yield to worst" is. That amount is the yield you will receive if the bond is called early.

It may seem a little intimidating, but purchasing municipal bonds is not that difficult when purchased from reputable brokers. Ask them to explain everything to you. After you have done one or two transactions, it will be relatively easy. It is certainly far easier than picking stocks.

Let me conclude with a word about bond funds. These are mutual funds that invest in bonds. They are often sold as though they are the same thing as investing in individual bonds. In reality they are quite different. They do not guarantee to repay your principal at maturity. The value of the bonds in the mutual funds fluctuates. When you sell, you may lose money on your original investment. I have been skeptical of bond funds since they were first popularized in the 1970s because they sacrifice the great benefit of bonds, which is an obligation by the issuer to repay your investment at a set maturity. Looking at the performance of the funds over time, my skepticism has proven correct, with the possible exception of junk bond funds, which are inappropriate for beginning investors.

STOCKS

I recommend investing in stock index funds because all of the studies that have been done show that they outperform most managed stock funds over the years.[81] They generally do not have front- or back-end loads (purchase fees that incur when you buy or sell), and they have low, minimum-investment requirements. Index funds have a high degree of diversity because they hold shares in all of the companies in the index. For example, the Standard & Poor's 500 index has five hundred stocks in companies with the largest market capitalization, so the Vanguard 500 index fund indirectly gives you shares in all of these five hundred companies. Of course, the index funds mirror the market capitalization of the stocks in

---

81. *See, The Index Funds Win Again*, THE NEW YORK TIMES, February 21, 2009. (Reporting on a very recent study by Mark Kritzman of Windham Capital Management showing that it is "extremely rare" for a managed mutual fund or hedge fund to beat an index fund after taxes and fees.)

the index. So you have a greater share in the most expensive and widely held stocks. This weighting of market capitalization tends to diminish the diversification somewhat. Still, if you compare your diversification in an S&P 500 index fund with investing on your own, you will readily see that there is vastly more diversification in an S&P Fund.

There is an additional benefit to index funds, which bears some consideration. Index funds spend very little on administrative expenses compared with managed mutual funds. This savings gives the index funds an important edge over managed funds, which typically spend up to 2 percent per year on advertising and managers.

Index funds work because they do not depend on insight or analysis. They depend on the general direction of the market, which has—notwithstanding its recent problems—historically been upward over many years. They also work because they do not cost as much to run. They only require a computer program and a few people to administer the fund. Unlike most mutual funds, they do not consume a lot of your money with so-called "research." Virtually every study over any great length of time has shown that they outperform at least 90 percent of the investment gurus. So if, like most of us, you are not a guru in the upper tenth of your class when it comes to stocks, buy the indices.

Index funds can be purchased from any number of brokerage houses. You can buy them from Vanguard, the pioneer of index funds, or you can buy them in your brokerage account as "exchange traded funds." These "ETFs" can be bought and sold like stock.

Choosing an index in which to invest is another challenge. Traditionally the most popular index has been the

Standard & Poor's 500, and the most popular fund has been the Vanguard 500 Index Fund, which tracks it. This index has worked well, but it is less diversified than the index funds that track indices comprised of more stocks. Obviously the more diversified you are, the less risk you have. If you want EFTs, Diamonds (symbol DIA) track the Dow Jones 30 industrials, SPDRS (symbol SPX and pronounced like the insects) track the S&P 500, and Vanguard Total Market Index VIPERS (symbol VTI) track 1,200–1,300 stocks traded on the New York Stock Exchange and the NASDAQ market. Additionally, for dividend yield, I recommend the Dow Jones Select Income Fund (symbol DVY), which is an index fund of carefully selected high-dividend-paying companies in the Dow Jones average. Finally, if you are looking for some foreign exposure, EFA tracks the MSCI EAFE index of large industrial companies based in developed countries other than the United States and Canada.

While we are on the subject of dividend-paying stocks, I would like to point out my strong preference for investing substantial amounts of money in dividend-paying stock indices or even, in some cases, the stocks themselves. According to Standard & Poor's, more than one-half of the approximately 10 percent return of the S&P 500 since 1926 has come from dividends. Dividend-paying stocks are generally far less volatile, particularly in down markets. If you want to control risk, companies that pay a healthy dividend and have increased their dividend every year are the companies in which you want to invest. In addition to DVY discussed above, you can consider the S&P Utility Stock Index, which can be purchased as an ETF with the symbol IDU.

Buying individual stocks is fun, but it is not likely to make you as much money as you would think. First, there is a great deal of research that must be done to pick a stock. Brokers are often wrong in their picks despite their supposed expertise. Second, even if you use a discount broker, transaction costs are significant. Third, despite all the efforts of regulators since the 1930s, you will not have access to timely information that Wall Street professionals have. They will be in and out of the stock while you are still buying on some positive news. If you still want to "play the market," here are a few rules:

1. Do your research. Invest only in high-quality companies with a proven track record of growth. Do not sell the stock unless something really goes wrong that signals that the company will be in a prolonged decline. If you hold stock in good companies, eventually the value will increase. Beware of brokers who urge you to sell quality companies they recently urged you to buy. They will get rich on commissions; you will lose.

2. If your stock goes down, consider buying rather than selling. Remember, if you liked a stock at $75 per share, you should like it even more at $65 per share, assuming that the underlying story of the company remains the same.

3. Do not trade in options. They are too complicated for most of us to understand, and the transaction costs are too high. Options involve a high degree of risk. The only exception is the writing of "covered calls" on the stock you hold in which you agree, for an amount of cash paid to you when you write the call, to surrender the stock at an agreed price higher than the current price for a limited period of time. When you write a call, you agree to limit your upside potential in a stock you own for some money, which you receive for writing the call. The call is considered "covered" because it is written on stock you already own. Your risk is not very great in this scenario.

4. Do not try to time the market. Nobody ever times it correctly. If the stock is worth buying at the current price, buy it at, or a little below, the market price. Do not set excessive limit orders (limiting the price at which you will buy or sell), although setting limits on your orders is always appropriate.

5. Try to invest your money on a "dollar cost averaging" basis. That is, don't invest all of your money at once. Invest a fixed amount on a monthly or quarterly basis. This way you will minimize the effect of market swings on your portfolio.

6. Do not invest in currency or commodities. It simply is not worth the risk.

7. Do not invest on "margin," where the brokerage house lends you money against your stock. This game will leave you vulnerable to losing your shirt if the stock goes down and the brokerage house forces you to sell stock in your account or post more collateral to cover your margin loan. Moreover, the cost of the loan makes the investment quite expensive and makes it more difficult to make a profit. Remember, margin is leverage, and excessive leverage is precisely what has caused our current economic problems. If professionals cannot manage leverage, you will be unlikely to succeed at it.

8. Do not invest in commercial real estate. It is compli-cated and time consuming. Additionally, such investments are not easy to liquidate when you need to cash in your chips. It is better to invest in real estate investment trusts ("REITS"), which do all the work and pass through the gains to you. There are many REITS that are publicly and actively traded. In con-sidering investing in REITS, you should always bear in mind that if you own a home, you have already invested a large por-tion of your assets in real estate. That real estate represents a

substantial risk in your portfolio. Thus you should be careful not to overweight your portfolio with real estate.

Please understand that the key to winning in the investment business is to understand risk. You must know how much risk you are willing to take and how much risk you are actually taking. Be sensible, and do not take a huge risk with your portfolio. Such risk is not necessary to achieve your goals. When you are young, you can take some risk with up to one-half to three-fourths of your portfolio. And it is not unreasonable for you to invest in a small amount of higher risk investments. But often that higher risk investment is simply an investment in your law firm or your house.

On the issue of risk, some people, including leading pundits of personal finance, believe (or at least want to believe) that the stock market is the only place to invest. I disagree. In some years, the stock market produces 30 percent gains, but do not fool yourself. Such gains, as we have painfully seen, come at a price in terms of risk. Actually, historically the stock market has only returned about 9 percent per year. Although current rates are a bit lower, you can generally obtain a 5 percent insured CD or municipal bond with virtually no risk. So in my opinion, a substantial portion of your portfolio should be placed in CDs or bonds. You will preserve your capital, and if you reinvest the interest you receive, the power of compounding interest will increase your savings substantially.

401(K) PLANS

If your firm offers a 401(k) plan, invest as much as you can in the plan. The tax deferral of investment gains on such a plan over the course of your career is a dramatic benefit. If your firm contributes to the plan, it is even better.

Often I hear from lawyers who say they cannot invest in the 401(k) because they do not have any money. This excuse is flimsy. When the government and perhaps your firm are subsidizing you, you cannot afford to pass up the opportunity. Remember, too, the tremendous power of compounding in a tax-deferred environment. Over time, a small amount of money can become a huge amount if invested and reinvested wisely.[82]

If your firm does not provide a 401(k), you can still obtain tax savings from standard IRAs, which involve contributions that are currently tax deductible, and Roth IRAs, the income from which is tax free.[83] Use them. The small reduction in your standard of living today will result in your being able to support yourself in much greater comfort when you are older.

HOUSES

Notwithstanding the recent decline in home values, a house is usually a good investment, not only because the government

---

82. An added feature of retirement accounts is that they are exempt from creditors. You will probably not have a judgment entered against you, but if you do, creditors cannot touch your retirement money.

83. IRAs come in two types. The first are regular IRAs, in which your contribution is immediately tax deductible and on which you pay income tax when you eventually take out the contribution and earnings. The second are "Roth IRAs," in which you get no tax deduction for your contribution, but the earnings and your contribution will come out tax free. The Roth IRA is excellent, but eligibility to use it is subject to income limitations. For example, in 2009, only single filers with "modified adjusted gross income" ("MAGI") of $116,000 or married persons filing jointly with MAGI of $169,000 could qualify at all. The full contribution was available only to single filers with MAGI of no more than $101,000 or married joint filers with MAGI of $159,000.

subsidizes it with income tax deductions (interest and taxes)[84] and tax-free rollovers when you invest in a new house, but also because it is a forced savings plan, which you can enjoy. Early home ownership generally leads to a more prosperous lifestyle. In fact, I can remember at least one year in which I made more on my house than I did at work. Generally, in terms of the investment value of your house, you should select the least expensive home in the most expensive neighborhood you can afford. This selection will maximize your return when you sell it. Remember that most people live in houses for only seven years before trading them in. So looking at the investment growth of the house is important.

In choosing a neighborhood, you should seek neighborhoods with the most consistent historical overall appreciation. Schools and taxes are important considerations, but not necessarily the determinative ones. Get information from real estate agents and, if necessary, from the public records to help you analyze your investment. One popular source is http://www.zillow.com, where you can obtain useful estimates of value.

Be careful about mortgages. Contrary to popular belief, real estate mortgages are not necessarily a cheap way to borrow money. However, you will probably be stuck with one. Here are a few pointers.

A fifteen-year mortgage is usually a better deal than a thirty-year mortgage. The interest is lower, and you will build

---

84. As I write, Congress has extended a temporary $8,000 tax credit for qualified first time home buyers, which has been an important part of the economic stimulus package. It is doubtful that this particular benefit will become permanent, but the enactment of the credit reflects the general desire of the government to subsidize home ownership.

up equity in your home more quickly. All the excuses about the higher monthly payments do not change this hard truth. If you must have a thirty-year mortgage, I recommend that you supplement your payment every month with an additional amount of money to pay off the principal early. You will save a vast amount of money.

You will undoubtedly encounter the question of whether to pay "points," the fee charged by banks to originate loans. Normally everyone is attracted to "no points" deals. However, check on the total cost. It may be worth paying some points to obtain a reduced rate of interest. This is especially true if you intend to live in the house and pay the mortgage for a long period of time.

A word about adjustable rate and "balloon" mortgages is in order. I recommend against these devices because they tend to make it easier to outspend your resources, and they involve a bet on future interest rates. If the current economic crisis has shown us anything, it is that even the best investment advisors cannot predict the future course of economic events.

AUTOMOBILES

Everyone buys automobiles and most of us aspire to having a good one. But the cost of buying and maintaining an automobile is substantial and will have a significant effect on your ultimate wealth.

My suggestion is to buy a car principally on the basis of (a) safety, (b) its cost to maintain, and (c) its ability to retain its value over time. All this information is available in *Consumer Reports*, the *Kelley Bluebook* (available at http://www.kbb.com), and http://www.safercar.gov.

When buying a car, do a lot of comparative shopping. You will find dealers in locations outside your immediate area will often give you their best prices over the telephone. If possible, negotiate *down* from the "invoice" price, which you can obtain online from *Kelley Bluebook*.

Consider buying a slightly used car. Many dealers can provide you with a substantial factory warranty. You can save a lot of money without sacrificing quality.

Do not lease the car. This is almost never a good deal. Buy the car and hold it for at least ten years. If you own and hold the car for ten years, you can afford to buy quite a luxurious car, assuming that its maintenance cost is low.

I know that you may be one of those who believes in trading cars often and only thinks about the monthly payment. But please, if you do the math, you will see that you will be much better off following the advice I have given you to avoid leasing and trading. You can save tens of thousands of dollars, which can be put to much better use.

BAD INVESTMENTS

Finally, these are the investments you must always avoid:

1. Any investments based on "inside tips." Such investments may be illegal.

2. Any investment that you do not understand thoroughly. If it is too complicated, don't buy it.[85]

3. Any investment in whole life insurance; term life insurance is adequate.

4. Any investment in commodities. It is a type of investment that is too volatile and risky.

---

85. That includes variable annuities and derivative products from insurance companies. If Wall Street bankers had followed this advice, we would have avoided incalculable damage.

5. Any investment in options (except covered calls) because they are also too risky.

6. Any investment in foreign bonds because they involve currency and other risks that require too much expertise for you to understand.

INSURANCE

Insurance is a necessary part of the investment plan. If you don't protect yourself and your assets, you may well be wasting your time investing.

Every young lawyer should have life and disability insurance. To become disabled or to die when you are young is tragic, but it is even more catastrophic if you have no insurance. Your family will have no support, particularly in the early years when your children are young. If you become disabled, you may have no means of support other than a pittance from Social Security. So do not squander your good health and youth. Buy insurance while you are still insurable and keep it in force.

Life Insurance

Life insurance comes in all varieties, and you will be swamped by salespersons with all sorts of proposals involving "whole life" investment policies. These policies pay a rate of return and have a "cash surrender value." Some of the policies, such as variable rate annuities, tie the rate of return to the stock market, letting you entrust your hard-earned money to the "wise" insurance company to invest. My advice is to limit yourself to term insurance, which simply pays money if you die.[86] This life insurance is the cheapest kind avail-

---

86. If you have dependents, the amount should be about twenty times your annual income.

able and lets you keep your money to invest yourself. Whole life policies are of value only if you cannot save and need a periodic bill to force you to build up your savings. If you are looking for life insurance, try the Internet. For example, http://www.selectquote.com is an excellent site to find cheap policies.

Disability Insurance

According to a Gallup survey conducted for one of the leading disability insurance carriers, if you are under the age of thirty-five, the chances are one in three that you will be disabled for at least six months during your career. Men were found to have a 43 percent chance of becoming disabled during their working years. *At age forty-two, it is four times more likely that you will become disabled than that you will die during your working years.*[87] So if you believe in insuring your life, you have to believe in insuring against disability.

Disability insurance, unfortunately, is very expensive. It is best purchased through a group. There are different types of policies. Some cover partial disability. Some cover total disability. Some cover disabilities that are total and then become partial or "residual." Some cover you if you are sufficiently incapacitated that you cannot return to your "own occupation." Some require that you be a vegetable to collect.

Look for "own occupation" policies; these cover you if you cannot practice the type of law you used to practice. So-called "total disability" policies may not pay you if you can still work at a minimum wage occupation.

---

87.   As cited at http://www.protectyourincome.com, last visited June 25, 2009.

Disability policies all have an "elimination period," which varies from as little as seven days to as long as six months. Obviously the longer the elimination period, the lower the premium. If you are paying, you should take a longer elimination period. Increasing the elimination period will reduce the likelihood of your making a claim (most disabilities are resolved within six months), but the savings will be worth it.

The taxation of disability payments is also a vital issue. If you have paid for the premiums yourself with after-tax dollars, the disability payments are not taxable. If your firm has paid the premiums, they are taxable. This difference is enormous.

Medical Insurance

You should carefully examine your medical insurance. Today this insurance is the single most important aspect of your financial planning, although while you are young you might not think so. One catastrophic health crisis and you can be wiped out. Getting decent insurance while you are young and healthy is important.[88]

Your firm may offer you a choice between HMO and PPO coverage. Straight indemnity insurance is, sadly, a thing of the past. HMO coverage is the least attractive. You are limited in the providers you can see and when you can see them. A "gatekeeper" doctor typically has to agree to send you to a specialist before you can see one. The gatekeeper, however, may have an undisclosed financial or other incentive to delay the referral. Moreover, the process of consulting with a gatekeeper is time

---

88. As I write, Congress is in the process of considering major changes in the manner in which medical insurance is delivered. It is difficult to predict what will come of these changes, if any are made. However, what I write here should be read in light of such changes.

consuming, frustrating, and sometimes counterproductive to your health. By contrast, a PPO plan gives you greater flexibility in the type of doctors you can see within the PPO network and gives you the option of going outside the network for treatment at a higher cost.

In looking at a PPO, you should look at the network not only in your community, but also outside of it. Look at whether major medical centers such as the Johns Hopkins Medical Center, Cleveland Clinic, Mayo Clinic, and Memorial Sloan Kettering Cancer Center are on the plan. Insurance is for catastrophes, so think about whether your insurance really provides for handling catastrophes rather than providing low-cost, palliative care to healthy people.

One vital aspect of health insurance is not usually addressed by financial planners: the amount of lifetime coverage you should buy. All policies have upper limits on the coverage they provide. Typically, such a limit might be $2 million. At today's costs, you can blow through a $2 million cap. So look for at least a $5 million cap. If you cannot find insurance with a high cap, or if your firm does not offer it, I urge you to consider carrying a catastrophic health policy, a policy, for example, with a deductible of $25,000. That way, if disaster strikes, you will not be wiped out financially.

Auto Insurance

Auto insurance is extremely important. If you are at fault for a serious accident, you can lose all of your assets. Of equal concern is the possibility that you may be the victim of an auto accident caused by an uninsured or underinsured motorist. If you are severely injured, you may have a hard time getting the health care and rehabilitation you need.

Today auto insurance is easily priced online. You should maintain liability coverage sufficient to meet the requirements of your umbrella coverage discussed below and provide sufficient uninsured motorist ("UM") coverage.

The importance of UM coverage cannot be overstated. In many parts of the country, it is common for drivers to maintain little or no insurance. If one of them hits you, you will receive no compensation if you do not have UM.[89] Buy as much UM coverage as you can reasonably afford. What makes you valuable as a lawyer is precisely what makes this type of insurance as important as life insurance.

Homeowner's Insurance

Homeowner's or renter's insurance is essential not only to deal with the loss of your own belongings through fire or theft[90] (which in the beginning of your career might not be worth very much), but also to deal with a variety of other exposures with which you are probably unfamiliar. For example, if someone is hurt in your home (e.g., by tripping on a rug), your homeowner's insurance will probably cover it. If you are walking down the street in a blinding rain storm and you poke your umbrella in someone's eye, the homeowner's or renter's policy will provide protection, not only against the risk of a judgment, but also against litigation costs.

---

89. Of course, there is some argument that UM coverage is redundant of disability and health insurance. However, if you become disabled, you may not be able to maintain your health insurance. Moreover, health coverage is limited, particularly in cases of severe and lasting injury. As for disability coverage, it is helpful, but it is generally limited to 60 percent of your income. So the additional protection of UM is, in my view, well worth it.

90. In some parts of the country it is necessary to obtain separate supplemental policies to cover wind, flood and earthquake perils.

Umbrella Coverage

Umbrella policies provide extra limits for liability for non-commercial torts that you commit, but which are not covered by primary insurance such as auto or homeowner's insurance. They are easily obtained at reasonable cost and typically boost your coverage for liability to $1 million or more. Unless you have extensive assets, I recommend carrying an "umbrella" policy of $5 million. The policy may—depending on where you live—enable you to increase your UM coverage and decrease your underlying primary insurance limits. Your insurance agent can explain it in greater detail to you, but it is important if you want to preserve your assets.

Malpractice Insurance

Malpractice insurance is extremely important to all professionals. Your firm should provide a sufficient amount of this insurance, but it is wise to make a discrete inquiry if you have a doubt. A larger problem arises if you change firms. You have to be certain that the old firm's policy is going to cover your past acts or that the new firm's policy will. Therefore you should ask so that, if necessary, you can purchase appropriate "tail coverage."

Travel Insurance

Before you travel outside the United States, learn whether your medical insurance will cover you. If not, travel insurance is easily obtained from http://www.travelguard.com and similar Internet sites.

Not covered in most travel insurance is the risk of kidnapping. For most people, it will not be an issue. But if you travel to certain foreign countries, it is now highly desirable to purchase a policy to provide for the payment of ransom and the services of trained negotiators to help free you.

Where to Buy Insurance

The best place to buy life, homeowner's, and car insurance today is on the Internet. The old days in which the insurance agent bonded with his customers and provided real service are, regrettably, over. While I still like the comfort of advice from my insurance agent, the reality is that this same advice is available online or over the telephone from most reputable companies.

You can find medical insurance on the Internet as well. In this connection, your state insurance regulator may have a site that is helpful in identifying companies writing in your state. Malpractice insurance is available through bar associations and agents. You may find it helpful to shop around.

If you follow the program I have outlined, I cannot guarantee that you will end up rich. However, you will maximize your chance of attaining financial independence, a worthwhile and reasonable goal. Although the program is somewhat more conservative than most investment advisors recommend, I think that it is well designed to avoid disaster and to take advantage of the current incentives available in the financial system.

TIPS FOR DEALING WITH YOUR SPOUSE OR SIGNIFICANT OTHER

Spouses or significant others bear an exceptional burden in a relationship with a lawyer. There are no easy answers to the issue of maintaining your relationships, but here is some advice that has worked well for my wife and me.

1. Help your spouse recognize the stress under which a new lawyer labors and explain that the stress is combined with the exhilaration of learning a new trade and perfecting your skills. When I was newly married, I was assigned to a major litigation, which consumed extreme amounts of time. In fact, the only way my wife could have dinner with me was to come to my office so we could go out to have Chinese food across the street. I was working at least 18/7. My poor bride was in tears, thinking that my firm was torturing me. She did not understand that this was the most exhilarating time of my life and

that the case was the opportunity of a lifetime. For my part, I did not do a good job of communicating the requirements of my job, the thrill of working on such an important case, or the necessity of my wholehearted commitment to the process. Things improved once I explained that it was not all drudgery and the case would not last forever.

2. Take a moment every day to speak with your spouse by telephone and convey how important he or she is to you. Once a day for a few minutes is enough. It doesn't hurt to ask, too, if there is something you can pick up at the store on the way home.

3. Introduce your spouse to the other lawyers in the firm. It is a good way for spouses to feel they are part of the process. Usually, meeting the people in the firm involves getting together socially with colleagues and their spouses or partners.

Young people tend to shy away from entertaining senior lawyers because they are naturally intimidated (and because older lawyers may be boring), but I have found that a more senior lawyer and his or her significant other are often interested in meeting younger people. Not everyone over the age of fifty feels ancient. Cast a wide net.

4. Set limits on your work. Even a Type A personality must set limits to achieve success. While a vacation may have to be rescheduled to accommodate a changing trial date, it cannot be deleted like a computer file. Lawyers should come home from work at a reasonable hour and spend quality time with their families. If necessary, additional work can be done from 10:00 p.m. to midnight, or later if needed. Even my father, who was an incredibly hard worker, started work at 8:00 a.m., came home at 5:00 p.m. every day, and then spent four hours with us, before working from 9:00 p.m. to 3:00 a.m.

5. Try to focus on improving the quality of life at home. While some talk about the problems of the workday is natural, it can become a negative experience for both spouses. Set a time limit on it. In the end, there is nothing you can do about the problems of work over dinner. Use the time to solve the family's problems, not the firm's problems.

6. Be sure to spend at least one evening a week and one weekend a month with your spouse or family alone. If you allow the clutter of demanding lives to crowd out your marital life, your marriage cannot last.

While law is a demanding mistress, it must never be allowed to interfere with your family life to the degree that that life is jeopardized. It is particularly important to avoid dividing labor with your spouse to such an extent that you begin to lead separate lives. A Type A lawyer can come into work early enough to be able to get home to see his son's baseball game or to help take a child to a piano lesson. By consciously avoiding a complete division of labor in your household, you will find that you have a much closer relationship with your spouse and your children.

Finally, I want to say a special word about children. It goes without saying that nothing in life is more important than the time and energy you devote to your kids. If you fail to devote enough time to kids, you will not save yourself any time or money. You will suffer enormously, as will they. You probably will spend years with expensive therapists trying to correct the problems that you have created. Spend the time early on. It is the best investment you can make, and it will enhance your career rather than detract from it.

ALTERNATIVE PATHS

The greatest thing about law is that you can reinvent yourself many, many times. Indeed, creative lawyers reinvent themselves every day. Many people start down a career path and decide they need a change. The profession allows you to make such changes. Many of your basic skills are transferable. Others can be acquired by a skilled lawyer. In my own career, I have been a litigator, but I started out as a tax lawyer. I have had many subspecialties in litigation, while practicing in many different environments.

Just to give you an idea of how diverse a range of opportunity awaits you as you develop your career, let me give you a few examples from what I have seen over the years:

1. *Establishing a privately funded public interest firm.* David Lansner and Carolyn Kubitschek established a public interest law firm in New York City, which is a successful for-profit firm funded largely by fee-awards in civil rights cases.

2. *Working offsite.* Axiom advertises itself as a firm for companies looking to enhance their in-house capabilities with an outside lawyer who will come to the company and help them manage complex legal issues. Axiom prides itself on excellent attorneys who want balance in their lives. It touts lower fees, based on reduced office expenses, since its lawyers work offsite.

3. *Working in the arts.* An associate with whom I worked became a concert promoter. He uses his legal skills to manage a charitable fund for the arts.

4. *Becoming an investment banker.* Several former colleagues of mine became successful investment bankers.

5. *Becoming a judge.* A number of my former colleagues have become well-known judges.

6. *Becoming a politician.* A few of the lawyers with whom I have worked have become successful politicians. Even those who have failed to be elected have found enormous reward in the process of running for office.

The strategic choice of which path to follow in your evolving career is always challenging. However, opportunities abound for you as your career unfolds.

I would suggest that the most important thing you can do when changing directions is to think about creating options. Ask yourself whether the change you make now creates more opportunities for change you might want to make in the future. The goal should be to expand options rather than to contract them, particularly in the early part of your career.

Money is an important factor to consider when making a change, but it is not an end in itself. You did not choose to be a lawyer because it could make you rich. You chose law because you wanted to do the work of law. So if you are tired of your job, or if the job is not as challenging as you want it to be, don't be afraid to make a change. The days when you could pass the bar and then work in one firm for your entire career are largely gone. At the same time, the barriers to creative possibility have also fallen.

I do not suggest that you change your area of law every year. Indeed, there is a penalty for giving up one expertise for another. All I am saying is that you are not a slave. You have a great deal of freedom with your law degree to pursue new avenues.

Change often produces great results for lawyers. I have seen many lawyers who did not find a good fit with their firms move to other firms in which they flourished. Many lawyers move from the private sector to the public sector, where they find new opportunities for professional development. Indeed, Washington, D.C., is a place where change of this sort is extremely frequent.

Not unlike divorces, of course, change can involve cost. When you move from one firm to another, some clients will stay with the old firm, but the change of platform may well give you a competitive edge. Spending a few years in the government can remove you from the world of clients and make it difficult to rebuild your practice. At the same time, you have the opportunity to develop and sell a new range of skills and connections.

The most important thing to remember about changing careers in the law is that it should involve thought and calculation of the benefits and detriments of the move. Too often I have seen lawyers who did not think through the consequences of their hasty decision to give up one kind of practice for another. They ended up in a worse position.

It is often wise when making decisions about career changes to consult with professionals. There are consultants and career coaches in the law who can be of help. You will find many lawyers who will be happy to help you as well. Above all, keep an open mind. As long as you have your health, endless opportunity awaits you.

THE FUTURE OF THE PROFESSION

We have covered a lot of ground in this short book. However, we have really not discussed one of the most important subjects from the perspective of a new lawyer: what are the future trends of the profession? Such trends are important, of course, because it is important to think strategically about your career from the outset. Future trends are also important because you may be able to contribute to a greater degree to the development of the profession if you can grasp them early on. What I am going to say, though, is simply a prediction. You and your peers will determine its validity by your professional work.

THE EXPANSION OF LAW

At the outset, we need to step way back and look at an overall trend in modern Western societies, which was identified and described well by the famed German lawyer and sociologist Max Weber. Weber, writing in the early twentieth century, identified a trend toward ever-increasing "rationalization" and bureaucratization of modern societies through the development of ever-more-sophisticated, complex, and socially confining laws.[91]

Weber's prediction about the development of laws has been largely true in my lifetime. The Internal Revenue Code is now vastly larger than when I started practicing, and tax returns can only be prepared with a computer. The regulations promulgated pursuant to the Code have been expanded almost without end. The Federal Rules of Civil Procedure have grown more and more complex. The paperback version of The Federal Criminal Code used to be easily portable; now it is so heavy that it is cumbersome to lift. When I started practice, many law firms had complete sets of the *Federal Reporter*. Now the volumes are so numerous that most firms have given up trying to purchase them, relying instead upon Westlaw to store them.

It is likely that this long-term trend will continue during the course of your career. Thus you can be certain of three things at the outset:

1. The demand for lawyers will grow much faster than people now realize. The growth of law is not due to one political party or another; it is the inevitable growth of a modern society dedicated to the rule of law.

2. There will be a need for increased specialization on the part of lawyers in order to provide competent and efficient service.

---

91. *See generally*, MAX WEBER, THE PROTESTANT ETHIC AND THE SPIRIT OF CAPITALISM, TRANSLATED BY TALCOTT PARSONS (Dover Value Editions, 2003) (1904-5, Parsons trans. 1958).

3. The increased specialization will pressure lawyers to work in larger groups so lawyers can provide full service to their clients.

ECONOMIC TRENDS

Economics will continue to play a vital role in the law, as it does in the entire society. I am speaking here not only about the basis on which courts decide cases, but also about the structure of law firms and other legal organizations. Today everyone wants to know what will happen to the immediate economic life of law practice. In the very short term, we know that clients will be more price sensitive because of the current recession. But the recession will pass in a relatively short time. In planning your career, you have to look at the more distant horizon. So I am going to refrain from short-term predictions, even though the current recession may be a catalyst for economic trends that have already started and are likely to continue.

THE TREND TOWARD CONSOLIDATION

There has been a trend toward consolidation in the legal community. While there are still plenty of small firms and solos out there today, the percentage of lawyers working in large firms is growing rapidly.[92] The reasons for this growth are many. Larger firms bring in better clients with more profitable work. There is greater safety for the lawyer who works in a large firm because of the diversification of risk. If one practice area is in a slump, the chances are that another practice area will make up for it.

---

92. Marc Galanter and William D. Henderson, *The Elastic Tournament: A Second Transformation of the Big Law Firm*, 60 STAN. L. REV. 1867–69 (April, 2008).

There are many benefits for clients in using larger firms. In an age that demands specialization, large firms can provide full service to the client. If a lawyer becomes sick or dies, his clients can continue to receive legal services with minimal disruption.

Additionally, there are some relatively minor "economies of scale," or cost efficiencies, in larger firms. Such economies of scale, however, are not that great because of the emergence of information technologies, which have enabled the small firm to produce work at the same or lower cost.

The trend toward merger has grown exponentially in my career. Indeed, it was rare when I started practicing to see mergers. Over the past decade, however, it has become a constant aspect of the profession.

The trend of law firms to merge is likely to strengthen over time. Without market share, lawyers will have a tough time diversifying risk and negotiating fees with ever more demanding and sophisticated clients. Whether this trend is good or bad may depend on how the individual mergers are handled by the participants. One thing is certain: lawyers will be seen more as commodities or "production units" within firms than as "partners" and "colleagues."

In fairness, there are those who claim that the era of "Big Law" is over. Richard Susskind, a British critic of the legal industry, has argued that new and "disruptive" information technologies will spell the end of the large corporate firms as we have known them. Instead, he claims that they will be replaced by a few high-end boutiques providing customized services to a narrow group of clients who need such services, and a lot of individuals and companies utilizing standardized legal forms found on Web sites.[93]

I think, however, that while there will be further commoditization of legal work and the proliferation of standardized legal services, there will also be an increasingly creative expansion of law and complex business transactions requiring the services of highly trained humans capable of advising clients and negotiating. Litigation, of course, will always have a high degree of customization because it deals with a wide spectrum of factual and legal patterns. Standardization of contracts will not solve all of the complex legal needs of a prosperous society. The advent of Turbotax, after all, has not eliminated the accounting profession.

THE NEED FOR CAPITAL

Firms will require more capital. Initially the current recession will cause poorly capitalized firms to merge or to go out of business. In these financially difficult times, owners of weaker firms will be afraid to invest more in their firms. Eventually the better capitalized firms will emerge as winners. Emergence from recession, however, will not end the need for more capital to run law firms. Firms will learn that they need much more capital to grow and to sustain their viability. The growing demand for such capital will most likely lead to pressure on regulatory agencies to allow investment in law firms by non-lawyers and ultimately by the public through the capital markets.

---

93. RICHARD SUSSKIND, THE END OF LAWYERS? RETHINKING THE NATURE OF LEGAL SERVICES (Oxford University Press 2008). While I disagree with many of Susskind's conclusions, this provocative book has many valuable insights about technology and law. It is well worth reading.

Once capital is raised from sources outside the owners of private firms, the nature of law firms will change profoundly. The economics of the firms may stabilize, but their culture will come to resemble that of their corporate clients. Lawyers will view themselves more as employees than as owners. Managers are more likely to be professionals with business training. Indeed, one sees already that some large firms, driven by a cadre of professional managers, have engaged in ruthless layoffs of lawyers and non-lawyer support staff.

INCREASED COMPETITION

Overall we can expect greater competition in the legal market. Not only will there be more lawyers, but also many of the ethical rules that now hamper the movement of lawyers and methods of competition will be modified or eliminated. I am talking here about conflict-of-interest rules, fee-sharing rules, and laws permitting the enforcement of noncompetition agreements. These rules have traditionally given the profession the ability to reduce competition and increase prices.

As competition grows, firms will try to gain pricing power by increasing their size and market share. For example, if a client has a large case and needs a large firm to handle it, it will find that it has fewer choices and less bargaining power. While I do not foresee monopoly pricing, I believe that, as has occurred in the accounting profession, the large players will grow larger and their number will be dramatically reduced.

There will be plenty of smaller "boutique" firms, of course. Many will specialize in particular areas of the law. Many others will try to capture business, as they do today, by offering lower prices. These firms will deal with competition by increasing the quality of their service and/or the efficiency with which it is delivered.

COST REDUCTION AND LEVERAGE

All firms will have to deal with the issue of reducing costs. Here I foresee two alternative models, which will impact new lawyers differently. In the first model, firms will eliminate newer lawyers and provide services with a fewer number of more experienced lawyers willing to work without tenure for lower pay. This model will initially produce higher productivity and lower salary costs.

In the first model, firms can benefit by reducing, or even eliminating, their training costs. Eventually these firms could reduce their real estate costs by encouraging telecommuting and moving to less expensive offices. The advantage of having experienced professionals rather than new lawyers is that experienced lawyers can work successfully from their homes, while newer lawyers need closer supervision.

The first model will work to a degree, but it may not, ultimately, be as profitable to the owners as it might appear. However much they may try, firms following this model will not find a large enough pool of experienced lawyers who want to work productively for low wages over a long period of time. So the firms will have to pay the experienced lawyers more and more money. This increased cost will inevitably reduce "leverage." Using higher salaried lawyers to leverage law firms is like the owner of a taxi company trying to increase profit by enlarging his fleet of Mercedes Benz taxis. There may be some leverage, but unless all of his clients are millionaires unconcerned about paying high fares, increasing the size of the Mercedes fleet will not increase profit that much.

In the second model, firms will continue to recruit new lawyers, but attempt to increase their ability to profit from them. These firms will search for better methods of achieving "leverage." Initially firms pursuing this model will freeze, or reduce, associate pay. Given the cost of legal education, however, such actions will not be sufficient. If the pay is too low and student loans are too high, it will not be profitable for new lawyers to join these firms. This will be true particularly as firms cut back on training for which clients do not wish to pay.

To increase leverage, I believe that firms will want to hire more lawyers from lesser known and less expensive law schools. Eventually, however, pressure will be brought to bear on all law schools to turn the third year into a "clinical" training year in which students are given credit for working in law firms for little or no salary. The cost of training will thus be reduced at the expense of more costly theoretical education. Ultimately clients, firms, and students may even press for the elimination of the third year entirely to reduce the cost of legal education, although I can foresee a fierce battle over any reduction of the tuition necessary to maintain good schools.[94]

---

94. The battle has already broken out on the Internet with the posting of a highly provocative article in The Am Law Daily by Paul Lippe, a Silicon Valley general counsel and founder of Legal On Ramp, a Web site for corporate counsel. In the posting, Lippe argues that law schools are "complacent" and increasingly irrelevant to anyone other than their professors. He advocates an accelerated curriculum with one year of case study, one year of clinical study, and one year of externship. He suggests that lost revenue might be made up by schools offering specialized training to more experienced lawyers. *Welcome to the Future: Time for Law School 4.0*, http://www.amlawdaily.typepad.com/amlawdaily/2009/06/school.html, last visited August 14, 2009.

OUTSOURCING

Outsourcing to lower labor cost countries is one possible avenue of increasing leverage. Such globalization has already begun, and I believe that it will continue. There is no theoretical reason why a lawyer in Calcutta cannot learn American law and produce quality legal products. Numerous Indian lawyers are already doing American legal work, including document review and patent work.

Nevertheless, I do not foresee wholesale outsourcing of American legal jobs to the developing world at any time in the near future. There are obviously many impediments. Educational opportunity will limit the capacity of foreign lawyers to acquire American legal skills. Furthermore, knowledge of local American courts and admission to the bar in the United States are prerequisites to providing full services here. Malpractice, ethical, and other legal issues will continue to protect the franchise of American lawyers. And, of course, to some degree cultural differences will make it difficult for foreign lawyers to "take over" American jurisprudence.

LEGAL SALARIES

It is hard to predict what will happen to legal salaries. In the short term, there are clear signs that they are falling substantially, but the increased demand for lawyers that I anticipate will mitigate this downward trend somewhat over time. The Bureau of Labor statistics predicts that the number of lawyers will grow at a rate of 11 percent per annum through 2016, which is roughly the average for other occupations.[95] At the same time, I believe that the demand for legal services will

95.   *See,* statistics of the Bureau of Labor Statistics, available at http://www.bls.gov.

grow substantially. Thus salaries will tend to rise from whatever level to which they may fall in the current recession. How much they will rise is an open question. I think that the most we can say is what we have known for a long time: as an attorney, you will never become rich, but you will never starve. Indeed, as an entrepreneur, you may have the opportunity to take advantage of the emerging economic trends to significantly increase your wealth.

THE FATE OF THE BILLABLE HOUR

Much has been said about the supposed death of the billable hour as the unit by which we bill.[96] While I am certainly no fan of the concept that we bill entirely on the basis of time rather than value, I am skeptical that we can really escape the billable hour. Time is the most critical and scarce resource in our work. In some way, it has to be factored into any measurement of lawyer productivity. Even if we handle work on contingencies or flat fees, the amount of time we spend on a case is critical to determining whether the case was "worth it" and whether to take on further work on an alternative fee basis.

Nevertheless, while billable hours will still be essential to track, many clients will demand that we provide services that are, at least ostensibly, calculated on a basis tied more to achieving value and to meeting preset budgets. Such client demands will create opportunities for new business models for law firms that stress greater efficiency, achieved by well-

---

96.   For a thoughtful articulation of this view, it is well worth reading the address of Mark Chandler, the general counsel of Cisco, to the Northwestern School of Law's 34th Annual Securities Regulation Institute. http://www. blogs.cisco.com/news/comments/cisco_general_counsel_on_state_of_technology_in_the_law/ last visited August 13, 2009.

organized, highly motivated, and better-leveraged lawyers. If the fee is at risk from the outcome of the work, the work has to be of high quality. But a premium will be placed on the efficiency and low time cost of the work. In this connection, the development of knowledge management systems within firms will be important.[97]

SOCIAL STATUS VS. MERIT

Social status and ethnicity will continue to have some role in the legal profession, as they do in the society as a whole. But the trend is clearly toward a meritocracy. "Merit," however, will be judged less on the basis of paper credentials and more on the basis of efficient production of legal services at lower cost.

I believe that one positive aspect of this trend will be the decay of the "caste system," which has favored the graduates of the top twenty law schools to the detriment of graduates of other schools. The reality of American legal education today is that excellent education is available from many less famous schools whose graduates should be given greater consideration in hiring by all legal organizations.

INCREASED SIZE OF GOVERNMENT

In an increasingly "rational-legal" society, government grows. Whatever the merits or demerits of "big government," its constant growth throughout the history of the nation is a valuable predictor of what is to come. For lawyers, the growth of government means more jobs in both the public and private sectors, as well as more opportunities for lawyers to move back and forth between government and the private sector. The lack of training opportunities in large firms will provide impetus

97. *Id.*

for associates in such firms to seek on-the-job training in government agencies.

GLOBALIZATION

Globalization will only enhance the trends I have outlined. Many more firms will need to become global to handle the increasing number of transnational transactions in which their clients are involved. If you doubt the degree to which globalization affects American law, consider the sole practitioner who specializes in criminal law in a town in the Midwest. You would think that such a person would not be involved in international affairs. Yet a good portion of the clients of the Midwestern sole practitioner now come from foreign lands. The impact of these clients' criminal problems on their immigration status is a central issue in the representation. Many of their alleged criminal activities originate in or involve witnesses in foreign lands. No lawyer today can say that his or her practice is not impacted to some degree by the increasing velocity of international commerce.

CAREER LENGTH

It seems very likely that lawyers will enjoy longer careers in the future. The demographics of the "baby boom" generation will lead to decreasing retirement support from the government and the private sector. The cost of medical care continues to rise. It will be hard to retire in the future. Thus longer work lives will probably become the norm for the society. Already it is common for lawyers to work into their seventies. And although their productivity may be less, their experience and networking connections are, in many cases, quite valuable.

TECHNOLOGY

The role of technology in the future of the legal profession is an interesting one about which to speculate. Today we produce written work with far greater rapidity than when I started. In fact, at the first firm where I worked, lawyers dictated to live stenographers, and there was actually a typing pool of thirty typists continually typing and retyping drafts. Obviously technology has been a great help to us. At the same time, the ease with which we can duplicate forms has created the risk that work is not reviewed with the same care. In the area of legal research, computers have helped us enormously, but computers still cannot supplant manual labor and human thought.

What is certain about technology is that it is expensive. Information technology is a black hole into which we often blindly dump money and time. How much of your day is now spent on rebooting your computer, checking your e-mail, or texting friends and family? The trend here is clear: we are going to spend more time and money on technology. But will we increase our productivity? Without increases in productivity, we will become a poorer profession or else society will go broke paying us. Conceivably, specialization and consolidation will improve our productivity as a group, but the techniques I have outlined in this book will clearly be ever more important as time goes on.

I think there are four major issues with respect to technology that are important to keep in mind.

First, the Internet has made access to information much greater. This has led to the proliferation of standardized forms for those who cannot afford lawyers. For example, you can visit http://www.directlaw.com or http://www.legalzoom.com and find forms for setting up corporations, obtaining divorces, and handling many other legal transactions. For many individuals and corporations, standardized materials available through technology will reduce cost and eliminate the need for lawyers. As noted earlier, however, this will not in my view significantly impact the overall demand for lawyers because the law is becoming ever more complex. It requires specialists rather than do-it-yourselfers.

The second trend in technology is the great reduction in the cost of memory. This opens up great possibilities for storage and retrieval of data. For litigators, it makes it possible to utilize discovery rules to retrieve a vast amount of internal communication by parties to litigation. This tends to drive up the cost of litigation, although it may increase the accuracy of litigation outcomes by providing better evidence. For all lawyers, however, the reduced cost of memory makes it possible to create vast databases of legal knowledge within firms and on the Internet. It can ultimately lead to greater efficiency, although I remain skeptical that technology will produce gains in productivity in the legal profession on the level that has already occurred, particularly when it is netted against the rising cost of maintaining information technology systems.

The third issue that technology presents increasingly is the issue of security. It is now possible for malicious hackers to impair your computers, obtain data from them, and even utilize them as weapons for Internet attacks. This vulnerability is unfortunately true even when using so-called encrypted protocols for e-mail. Law firms will in the future have to spend ever-increasing amounts of money to protect against hackers and to repair damage from attacks. This will, in my view, further undermine the productivity gains that information technology may provide.

Finally, to end this section on a higher note, the development of information technology has and undoubtedly will continue to lead to better marketing and communication with clients, the courts, and other lawyers. Hopefully it can lead to collaborative sharing of ideas and improve the efficiency of many of the tasks that we perform. But don't worry! The era of the robotic lawyer powered by artificial intelligence is a long way off.

THE FUTURE OF PRO BONO

What about pro bono work? Unfortunately, I am less than optimistic about the future of pro bono work in private law firms. The competitive pressures I have described will make it increasingly difficult for private firms to dedicate as much of their resources to pro bono causes. I am, however, optimistic that more lawyers will devote portions of their careers to public service. Serving the public good has been a hallmark of our profession, and I cannot conceive of a time when this profession will abandon such a necessary and worthy ideal. Additionally, work in public interest organizations will provide good training at the same time that training will diminish in for-profit firms.

If the society moves toward ever-increasing governmental intervention, one would hope—at least ideally—that there will be greater government funding for legal aid services. Legal aid is usually one of the areas that is first to be cut in balancing budgets. However, as the government spends more money in general and as private firms become less able to contribute to legal aid services, we can expect some greater pressure on government to fund legal services. In an ideal world, the government subsidies for legal services might even carry over into subsidies for legal services to middle-class people, who are today unable to afford even basic legal advice.

THE QUALITY OF PROFESSIONAL RELATIONSHIPS

One disturbing trend I have seen in my career is the tendency of lawyers to engage in bitter personal disputes. Rather than focusing on the clients and their issues, lawyers increasingly turn everything into a contest between themselves. For example, prosecutors and defense lawyers often used to be friends and colleagues. Today prosecutors eagerly hope they can target defense lawyers for prosecution. Civil litigators increasingly look to damage their adversaries with motions for attorney sanctions based on discovery violations and unsupported pleadings. No doubt some of the rancor has been precipitated by real misconduct, but a lot of it has been generated by a decrease in "professionalism" and mutual respect among lawyers.

I do not glorify the "old days," when the "genteel profession" of law excluded women, gays, African Americans, Jews, and Irish Americans. However, at the same time that we are rightfully breaking down social barriers and increasing competition, we need to keep in mind that we cannot create a successful profession where the goal is to annihilate our adversaries at all cost. The lawyers of the future will need to be far more careful about the quality of their work and their personal conduct to avoid running afoul of the rules. Hopefully in the process they will also improve the collegiality of the profession.

In this connection, I note a greater tendency to reduce costs through the use of mediation to settle cases. At a time when lawyers are often cutting each other's throats, it is heartening to note that some lawyers, some clients, and the courts are pursing another agenda. Life does not need to be a zero-sum game in which one party wins at the expense of the other. If we can enlarge the concept of win-win solutions in our profession, we will, as Professor Seligman has suggested,[98] be happier lawyers.

I would like to be able to say that the legal profession will create a fairer and better society where equal justice is freely available to all. I do not, however, know whether that will be true, or whether lawyers will spend their time justifying repressive tactics by the government to smother our rights. That is for you and your generation to decide in a world that is ever more dangerous.

It is clear to me that in order to survive as a lawyer as the profession unfolds in the future, you will need every competitive edge I have tried to present in this book. Whether in the private sector or the public sector, you will want to think entrepreneurially. You will accomplish far more, and achieve greater professional and financial security, by improving the quality and efficiency of your service and marketing it in a sustained and effective manner.

---

98. Seligman et al., *supra* note 1.

WHAT ARE THE ATTRIBUTES OF A SUCCESSFUL LAWYER?

Becoming a leader of a legal organization should be related to becoming a successful lawyer, and to some degree it is. But it should be considered independently, since many fine lawyers do not become partners or the leaders of legal organizations. In reaching my conclusions, I have relied on my own observations, the observations of law firm leaders who have expressed their views to Vault Career Library,[99] and empirical study.

First and foremost, you have to decide for yourself what type of success you want to seek. Every lawyer has different objectives. One wants to make a lot of money. One wants to be a judge. Another wants to be a community leader. Yet another wants to run a law firm. All these, and many more, are valid objectives. What is significant, however, is that successful

---

99. VAULT, *supra* note 55.

lawyers achieve the objectives that they themselves define, and frequently redefine, as they progress.

Traditionally the expressed view has been that the brightest lawyer is the best lawyer. I have seen scant evidence in my career that this is true. Yes, brilliant lawyers are often very good, and they certainly have a leg up in competing for entry-level jobs in top firms. The lawyer who can analyze issues and write clearly about them on law school examinations can be a great lawyer. But it takes a lot more to be a *successful* lawyer. So if you are brilliant, you have a chance to be successful, but if you were not a brilliant law student, you will have every opportunity to outperform the smartest person in your law school class.

Success in the law and in life is based most profoundly on initiative. If you are the type of person who waits for an assignment, does it well, and waits for the next marching order, you will not succeed. You have to take ownership of the larger problem that the firm is confronting when it gives you an assignment. You want to assure senior lawyers and your clients that you have things under control or will take responsibility for the challenge of providing the service the client needs.

In your career development, you cannot sit back. It is important to take the initiative to motivate yourself in developing your skills as a lawyer and a marketer of yourself and your firm. This is true in any organization. The results may not be immediate, but they are certain over the longer haul.

Delegation is often encouraged, especially in large law firms. But in the early years, I recommend that you shoulder more responsibility. Delegation can sap initiative. It is not much of an answer to a client or a senior lawyer that you took a problem and assigned it to a junior lawyer who failed to turn in a properly executed assignment.

Closely related to initiative is a positive mental attitude. It is hard to take the initiative when you think that things are bad and will never get better. Successful lawyers always reformulate the difficult situations that they face in positive ways. Without dishonoring the importance of teasing out all of the problems that confront them and, more significantly, their clients, they find creative solutions. For every setback they face, they know profoundly that success is the best and only revenge.

Another prerequisite to success is sound judgment. To some degree, you are either born with this or you are not. But judgment can be learned by watching good lawyers, and it can be "outsourced" by seeking advice from colleagues whose judgments are more reliable.

Good interpersonal skills are also an important component of success. Clients and other parties are often under great pressure. Your ability to calm everyone down, to take charge, and to lead by example is extremely important. Regardless of politics, take as your model President Obama. Don't get too high when things go right or too low when they don't go right.

Praise others for their work and let them take credit for a good job. Don't get too down on people when they fail. Building up the pride of everyone is an essential interpersonal skill.

Within the interpersonal realm, I also include networking within and outside the firm. Leveraging your own strength with the strength of others is unbeatable and essential to success.

The ability to communicate effectively, both in writing and orally, is crucial, as is the ability to stay organized. If you have good organizational skills, a lot of good things happen. If you do not, don't expect much.

Lest you think I have nothing to back all this up, I recommend that you read Professor William D. Henderson's provocative paper, *Are We Selling Results or Resumes? The Underexplored Linkage Between Human Resource Strategies and Firm-Specific Capital.*[100] In it, he describes an elaborate two-year empirical study conducted many years ago by Bell Labs to determine the qualities found in their most successful performers. The top three were initiative, networking, and self-organization. What was striking about the study, however, was that cognitive ability and other "immutable traits" were not significant factors.

You can clearly learn to be a star performer.

---

100. *Supra,* note 5.

THE QUEST FOR EXCELLENCE

The quest for excellence in a legal career is a lifelong commitment to self-improvement, the improvement of other lawyers, and the improvement of legal institutions. It is not a quest for perfection. Many lawyers achieve outstanding results despite personal limitations. When Gerry Spence, whom I mentioned earlier, gives an opening statement, no one will miss the fact that he is not the most polished speaker and does not use the latest graphics to illustrate his arguments. What he has is the drive to prepare, prepare, and prepare. He is always the most knowledgeable person in the courtroom about the case at hand. He wins by working hard and helping to empower juries to give favorable verdicts to his clients. In short, preparation and hard work can turn a good lawyer into a great lawyer and a great lawyer into a brilliant lawyer.

Excellence in law begins by achieving a balance between personal life and work life. Such balance is not easy to attain, but it is essential. Those lawyers who have no personal lives have miserably failed themselves and their families (if they have them). To achieve a balance, good lawyers must be organized and motivated. If your relationships are bad or unsatisfying, get professional help. There are qualified people available to help you with insight into how to achieve good personal relationships.

Excellence involves something more than simply working hard, though some hard work is usually a prerequisite. Some lawyers work hard but have such poor judgment that their evident preparation renders their absurd conclusions and bizarre tactics frustrating and incomprehensible. Judgment in this context cannot always be taught. It may be a natural outcome of lifetime forces and experiences that cannot easily be changed. If you sense you are one of those lawyers with poor native judgment (or have friends good enough to tell you that you are), then you must reach out for the good judgment of others. Find someone with good judgment and run your problems and ideas by him or her. You will improve your judgment, even if you do not always take her or his advice.

Excellence in law involves integrity and honesty to a fault. The world is already convinced that lawyers are crooked, even though it is almost never true. You, therefore, have no leeway. Nor can you condone dishonesty on the part of those around you. How you respond to such dishonesty may be a complex question. Calling the police because a secretary makes a personal long-distance call on the firm's telephone is obviously excessive. But at the same time, you cannot let little things go without sacrificing your own integrity.

Excellence in the law involves proper respect for economic realities. The law is greatly influenced at all levels by economics. This means that first you must be productive and profitable for yourself and your institution. You cannot help achieve economically realistic goals for your firm and your clients if you cannot be economically realistic yourself.

Excellence in the legal profession involves strategic vision. You will profit enormously by spending the time necessary to plan your cases, your career, and your relationships in a way that leads to achieving goals you have set. It is also wise to identify your goals in every case and matter, even as we have seen the importance of establishing goals for your career and your life. Somehow lawyers forget this point, even though getting through law school certainly required such planning.

Excellence requires the ability and courage to "shift the paradigm." That is, you have to be able to change the way in which others look at a problem. For example, you do this as a litigator by taking the huge quantity of data that we call reality and organizing it in an innovative way that supports the objective of your advocacy. Even when the facts are against you, there is usually a way of marshaling them to the advantage of your client. As a transactional lawyer, your strongest skill should be the ability to find a way to accomplish a result that is beneficial for everyone concerned. Win-win solutions are the quintessential success of good lawyers.

Last, but not least, excellence in the law includes providing high-caliber service, not only to your clients, but also to the community in which you live. Good lawyers give good service. It is no coincidence that lawyers occupy a powerful position in American society. They have earned it by service in the courts, administrative agencies, legislatures, and charities since the birth of the nation.

Where lawyers often go wrong is in failing to be advocates for themselves. The society does not know what we do or how we have contributed to our country. The average working week for the country as a whole is about forty hours.[101] Lawyers will generally work between fifty and sixty. That is a major contribution to the productivity of the nation. When it is combined with the number of jobs lawyers have created for the society and the beneficial rules they have drafted for the society, it is easy to see why we are leaders. Without arrogance, we need to let people know that we are a selfless and dedicated group that makes a valuable contribution to their lives.

In changing times, there are many paths for success and enjoyment in the law. The uncertainties of change are always disconcerting. But a changing world is also an opportunity for creative and rewarding endeavor. I hope this book has been helpful to you, and I thank you for taking your precious time to read it. Good luck! I am rooting for you with confidence because I know that if you have come this far, you will undoubtedly succeed.

---

101.   *See,* Bureau of Labor Statistics, *supra,* note 95.

BIBLIOGRAPHY

BOOKS

Babcock, Linda and Laschever, Sara, *Women Don't Ask—Negotiation and the Gender Divide* (Princeton University Press, 2003).

Fisher, Roger, et al., *Getting to Yes* (Houghton Mifflin, 1981).

Foonberg, Jay, *How to Start and Build a Law Practice* (ABA 5th Ed., 2004).

Friedman, Lawrence M. *A History of American Law* (Simon & Schuster, 1973).

Lund, Morten, *Jagged Rocks of Wisdom* (The Fine Print Press, 2007).

Mnookin, Robert H. et al., *Beyond Winning* (Harvard Press, 2000).

Orman, Suze, *Suze Orman's 2009 Action Plan* (Spiegel & Grau, 2009).

Orman, Suze, *Women & Money: Owning the Power to Control Your Destiny* (Spiegel & Grau, 2007).

Orman, Suze, THE *Road to Wealth: The Money Book for the Young, Fabulous and Broke* (Riverhead Books, 2005).

Peratec Ltd., *Total Quality Management: The Key to Business Improvement* (Chapman & Hall, 1994).

Susskind, Richard E., THE *End of Lawyers? Rethinking the Nature of Legal Services* (Oxford University Press, 2008).

Vault, *View From the Top: Law Firm Leaders* (Vault Library, 2005).

Walton, Kimm Alayne, *Guerilla Tactics for Getting the Legal Job of Your Dreams* (Harcourt Brace, 1999).

Weber, Max C. E., THE *Protestant Ethic and the Spirit of Capitalism. Translated by Talcott Parsons* (Dover Value Editions, 2003) (1904-5, Parsons trans. 1958).

Wesemann, H. Edward, *The First Great Myth of Legal Management Is That It Exists* (AuthorHouse, 2004).

ARTICLES AND MONOGRAPHS

Beck, Susan, *Work Like an Egyptian*, NEW YORK LAWYER, January 29, 2009.

Catalyst, *Women in Law in the U.S.* (May 2009), available at http://www.catalyst.org, last visited September 9, 2009.

Calvert, Cynthia Thomas, *Reduced Hours, Full Success: Part-Time Partners in U.S. Law Firms* (The Project for Attorney Retention September 2009) available at http://nawl.org, last visited January 12, 2010.

Chandler, Mark, Address to Northwestern School of Law 34th Annual Securities Regulation Institute, http://www.blogs. cisco.com/news/comments/cisco_general_counsel_on_state_of technology_in_the_law/, last visited August 13, 2009.

Coleman, James E. and Gulati, Mitu, *Response to Professor Sander: Is It Really About Grades?*, 84 N.C. LAW REV. 1823 (2006).

Cotterman, James D., *Capitalization, Debt, and Taxes*, ALTMAN WEIL REPORT TO LEGAL MANAGEMENT, June 2000.

Daicoff, Susan, *Lawyer Know Thyself: A Review of Empirical Research on Attorney Attributes Bearing on Professionalism*, 46 AM. U. L. REV. 1337 (1997).

Eaton, William W., et al., *Occupations and Prevalence of Major Depressive Disorder*, 32 J. OCCUPATIONAL MED. 1079, 1081 (1990).

Galanter, Marc and Henderson, William, *The Elastic Tournament: A Second Transformation of the Big Law Firm*, 60 STAN. L. REV. 1867 (APRIL, 2008).

Gilson, Ronald J., and Mnookin, Robert H., *Sharing Among the Human Capitalists: An Economic Inquiry into the Corporate Law Firm and How Partners Split Profits*, 37 STAN. L. REV. 314 (1984–1985).

Goldberg, Elizabeth, *Is This Any Way to Recruit Associates?*, AM. LAW., August 2007.

Henderson, William, *The End of an Era: The Bi-Modal Distribution for the Class of 2008*, http://www.elsblog.org, last visited August 15, 2009.

The Index Funds Win Again, THE NEW YORK TIMES, February 22, 2009.

Henderson, William D., *Are We Selling Results or Resumes?: The Underexplored Linkage Between Human Resource Strategies and Firm-Specific Capital*, INDIANA UNIVERSITY SCHOOL OF LAW, RESEARCH PAPER NUMBER 105, APRIL 2008.

Henderson, William D., *An Empirical Study of Single-Tier versus Two-Tier Partnerships" in the AM LAW 200*, 84 N.C. L. REV 1691 (2005–2006).

Lippe, Paul, *Welcome to the Future: Time for Law School* 4.0, http://www.amlawdaily.typepad.com/amlawdaily/2009/06/school.html, last visited August 14, 2009.

Mamudi, Sam, *Rethinking Stocks' Starring Role*, THE WALL STREET JOURNAL, September 2, 2009.

NALP, *Women and Minorities in Law Firms by Race and Ethnicity*, NALP BULLETIN. http://www.nalp.org, last visited September 14, 2009.

NALP, *Market for Class of 2008 Law Graduates Shrinks,* available at http://www.nalp.org, last visited September 9, 2009.

NALP, *Law Firms Report More GLBT Lawyers, But Numbers Remain Small*, NALP BULLETIN, November 2008, http://www.nalp.org, last visited September 1, 2009.

NALP, *Minority Women Still Underrepresented in Law Firm Partnership Ranks—Change in Diversity of Law Firm Leadership Very Slow Overall* (NALP, 2007), available at http://www.nalp.org, last visited September 9, 2009.

The National Association of Women Lawyers, *Report of the Fourth Annual National Survey on Retention and Promotion of Women in Law Firms, October 2009*, available at http://nawl.org, last visited January 12, 2010.

Riskin, Leonard L., *The Contemplative Lawyer: On the Potential Contributions of Mindfulness Meditation to Law Students, Lawyers, and Their Clients,* 7 HARVARD NEGOTIATION L. REV.1 (2002).

Sander, Richard H., *The Racial Paradox of the Corporate Law Firm*, 84 N.C. LAW REV. 1755 (2006).

Seligman, Martin E. P., et al., *Why Lawyers Are Unhappy*, 23 CARDOZO L. REV. 33 (2001).